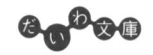

おにぎりレシピ101

山田玲子

JN201093

大和書房

今日はなんのおにぎり？

はじめに　INTRODUCTION

おにぎりは日本人のソウルフード、ヘルシーなファストフードです。

和食が世界で注目される中、おにぎりの知名度はお寿司にはとうてい及びませんが、「おふくろの味」とも言われ、日本の家庭料理の代表格です。

ご飯とおかずをにぎるだけのシンプルさ。

ご飯に合うものならなんでも美味しい。

組み合わせる具材は、国境を越え無限に広がります。

Onigiri — a healthy fast food — is the soul food of the Japanese.
Although it may not be as widely recognized as sushi, onigiri is synonymous with the phrase "taste of home," and is a staple of Japanese comfort food.
Its simplicity — just combining rice and toppings — offers endless possibilities without borders.

持ち歩き自由でどこでも食べられ、お弁当に、おやつに、夜食に、パーティーにとTPOに合わせて、どんなシチュエーションにも登場可能。

おにぎりは「おむすび」ともいい、手で「にぎる」「むすぶ」行為そのものを表す言葉です。

人は心を伝えるときに、手を繋いだり、握手したりします。手でにぎるおにぎりは、にぎる人の「気持ち」「温もり」という最高の調味料が加わり、美味しい「ごちそう」になります。

The portable onigiri can be served in all kinds of situations. It's perfect for bento lunch, as a light snack, or even as party food.
Onigiri is also called "Omusubi," which in Japanese means to bind or tie. When we make onigiri, we "bind" the rice together with our hands. Similarly, we hold or shake the hands of others when we express ourselves.
When onigiri is made by hand, the ball of rice is seasoned with the best ingredients — the warmth and love of the person who makes it — and transforms into a delicious meal.

目次 contents

1. 中に入れる FILL

2. まぜる MIX

目次
CONTENTS

3. 炊き込む／焼く　TAKIKOMI / GRILL

目次
CONTENTS

4. のせる／つつむ SUSHI-STYLE / WRAP

ご飯の炊き方
HOW TO COOK RICE

おにぎりには炊きたてのご飯が必要です。冷めたご飯ではおにぎりはにぎれません。ここでは、お鍋で簡単に美味しく炊けるご飯の炊き方を紹介します。

Always use freshly cooked rice since cold rice will not make a good onigiri.
Here are easy instructions on how to cook delicious rice.

1. お米を量る Measure the Rice

ご飯を炊くときは、お米と水の量は基本的に同量です（例えば、米カップ2：水カップ2）。

When cooking rice, prepare equal amounts of rice and water. For example, 2 cups of rice to 2 cups of water.

2. お米を洗う Rinse the Rice

ボウルにお米を入れて、たっぷりの水でざっと洗い流します。一度目の水はすぐにお米に吸水されるので手早く。再び水を入れ、手でさっとまぜてすぐに水を流します。同じ作業を二度繰り返します。

In a bowl, rinse the rice roughly with water. The rice will immediately soak up the first round of water, so rinse swiftly, and quickly drain the water. Repeat the process two more times.

3. お米を研ぐ Wash the Rice

お米がかぶる程度の水を入れ、お米の粒を壊さないように手でにぎるように洗います。5、6回やさしくにぎり洗いしてください。その後は再びたっぷりの水を入れ、3回ほど洗い流します。

Add just enough water to cover the rice. Rub the grains together by gripping the rice gently and thoroughly. Repeat 5 or 6 times. Add plenty of fresh water and rinse the rice about 3 times.

4. ざるにあげる Drain the Rice

研いだお米をざるにあげて、水を切ります。すぐに炊きはじめないで、水が完全に切れるまでおきます。

Drain the rice using a fine sieve and let it sit to make sure the water is completely drained.

5. 浸水させる Soak the Rice

お米と同量の水を鍋に入れ、30分おきます。お米の芯まで吸水させるためです。

Add the same amount of water as the rice into the pot. Let the rice sit and soak up the water for at least 30 minutes.

6. 炊く Cook the Rice

鍋を強火で炊きはじめ、鍋蓋から湯気が出はじめたら（沸騰したら）、弱火にして、10 〜 12分で炊きあがります。火からおろし、蓋をとらずに10分ほど蒸らします。

Heat the pot of rice with a lid over high heat and bring to a boil. When steam starts to seep out, reduce the heat to low and cook for another 10-12 minutes. Remove the pot from the heat with the lid still on. Let the pot steam the rice for another 10 minutes.

7. まぜる Mix the Rice

蒸らし終わったら、空気をふくませるように、お米をつぶさないようにざっくりとまぜます。

Take a rice paddle and swiftly, but gently, mix the rice as if folding in air between the grains. Be careful not to mash the rice.

塩のこと

塩はおにぎりになくてはならない大事なものです。

最初の一口での「美味しい」、これを決めるのが塩とその加減です。塩の味でおにぎりの美味しさが決まるといっても過言ではありません。

なぜおにぎりに塩が必要かというと、ひとつには塩は細菌の繁殖を抑える効果があり、ご飯の傷みを防ぎ保存効果をあげるからです。お弁当におにぎりは理にかなっているということです。

もうひとつは、塩がご飯と絡み合うとまとまりやすくなるからです。

そして、おにぎりを美味しくする秘密は手にあります。

私は手水をつけた後に、塩を手の平になじませてにぎります。

塩水を使う方もいますが、塩の塩梅をみるには手で塩の加減を

覚えることが大切です。なんども、なんどもにぎっていくうちに、手が塩加減、にぎり加減を覚えていくのです。

手水も手を濡らしすぎるとおにぎりは軟らかくなり、米粒はつぶれてしまいます。手水は少なめに取り、塩は親指、ひとさし指、中指の3本でつまむ程度の量がよいでしょう。

塩は、すぐに食べるときは軽く、時間をおいてから食べるときは、強めにつけてにぎります。塩のとり過ぎを敬遠して、おにぎりの塩を少なめにする方がいますが、ちょっと辛いかな……と思うくらいの量の方が形もまとまりやすく、ご飯となじんで塩の甘味

Salt is essential to onigiri. It's no exaggeration to say the salt and its amount determines how tasty an onigiri will be.

There are two reasons why salt is crucial. The first is its antibacterial properties, which prevents the rice from spoiling and allows us to preserve the freshness, making the onigiri perfect as portable lunch for bentos. The second reason is because the salt also serves an important role as the glue—sticking the rice together—to form a tight ball of rice.

The secret to making delicious onigiri however, lies in your hands. While others prefer dipping their hands in salted water before making onigiri, I usually wet my hands first, then gently rub some salt into my palms. This lets your hands "remember" and control the amount of salt. The more you mold the rice with your hands, the more you will understand, subconsciously, the ideal amount of salt and pressure to apply to the onigiri.

を感じることが出来ます。

炊きたてのご飯に天然塩をつけてにぎる。それだけでお米の甘みがぐっと引き立つのです。おにぎりに使う塩は、ミネラルが多く含まれる天然塩がおすすめです。

私は「わじまの海塩」（p.203参照）を使っています。輪島沖の100%海塩です。バランスのよい塩で素材になじみやすく、ご飯の旨味が引き立つ塩です。

おにぎりには日本の海水から作られた塩が一番合うと思いますが、自分好みの塩をいろいろと探してみるのも楽しいでしょう。

Be careful—too much water on your hands will flatten the rice and make the onigiri too soft.

Apply only a little bit of water and use your thumb, index finger, and middle finger to pick up a pinch of salt. Adjust the amount of salt to your preference, keeping in mind that more salt will preserve the onigiri for a longer period of time. Use less salt if the onigiri will be consumed immediately, and add more if later. Many have reservations about adding too much salt—but be generous. The salt will help the onigiri stay intact, and bring out the sweetness of the rice as it blends into the onigiri.

I recommend using natural salt with an abundance of inherent minerals. When applied to freshly cooked rice, it enhances the sweetness. My personal favorite is pure sea salt from the Wajima Shore called "Wajima Sea Salt" (see p.203). I'm biased for salt from the Japanese sea, but be adventurous and try out a variety of salt to find the perfect type for you.

おにぎりのにぎり方

HOW TO MAKE ONIGIRI

 ❶ 炊きたてのアツアツご飯を直接手にとってにぎるのは、慣れるまではむずかしいので、まな板など平らな面に一度とりおくか、お茶碗に軽くもります。

Take freshly cooked rice and put it into a bowl or on a cutting board to avoid burning your hands.

 ❷ 軽く手水をし、塩ひとつまみを片方の手にとり、両手をこすり合わせます。

Lightly wet your hands with water. Sprinkle a pinch of salt on your palms and rub them together.

 ❸ 手のひらに塩のつぶが少し残るくらいに塩をなじませます。

There should be some salt left on your palms.

❹ 丸くした手のひらにご飯をのせます。

Place some rice on your palm to hold the rice.

❺ もう片方の手をかぶせるようにおおい、力を入れすぎないようににぎります。

Cover the rice with your other hand, and firmly, but gently, squeeze the rice using both hands.

三角形 ［1個分：ご飯…100g／塩…適宜］
Triangular Onigiri ［100 grams of rice／some salt］

❶ かぶせる方の手を山型の三角にし、受ける方の手は厚みを整える役をします。

Cup the hand covering the rice sharply like a summit. The hand supporting the bottom of the rice will control the thickness of the onigiri.

❷ 三角形の一角ができたら、ご飯を60度手前に転がすようにし、3、4回転がし三角形に仕上げます。

To shape a neat triangle, rotate the rice 60 degrees with your hands 3-4 times and make the three corners of the onigiri.

❸ お米がつぶれてしまうので、何度もくり返しにぎらないようにしましょう。

Caution: Squeezing the rice too many times will crush the rice.

俵形 ［1個分：ご飯…50g／塩…適宜］
Tawara（Cylinder-Shaped）Onigiri ［50 grams of rice/some salt］

❶ ご飯をにぎるように持ちます。

Cup the rice firmly with one hand.

❷ もう片方の手で筒の両端を軽く押さえ、平らな面をつくります。

Use your other hand to squeeze and flatten the rice to make the ends of the cylinder.

❸ 俵形に形を整えながら、数回にぎります。

Mold the rice into a cylinder shape.

丸形 ［1個分：ご飯…50g／塩…適宜］
Round Onigiri ［50 grams of rice／some salt］

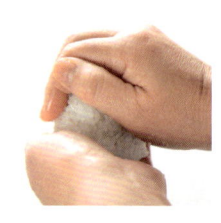

❶ 手にご飯をのせ、もう片方の手は角度をつけずに丸い形をつくってにぎります。

Place the rice into one hand. Cup your other hand and gently cover the rice.

❷ 丸く形を整えます。丸めにくいときは、ラップを使うと簡単にまとまります。

Mold the rice into a ball. If you find this difficult, try using saran wrap.

❸ 丸形を平らにしたい場合は、丸形を押しつぶすようににぎります。

For a coin-shaped onigiri, make a round onigiri then flatten the top and bottom.

おにぎりと具材の相性

ONIGIRI COMBINATIONS

「おにぎりに一番合う具は何ですか?」とよく聞かれますが、私はいつも「ご飯に合うものなら、なんでも」と答えています。

考え方のポイントとしては、

❶ しょっぱい味付け（塩、醤油、味噌、唐辛子など）

❷ 甘めの味付け（ソース、甘煮、ドライフルーツなど）

❸ 油っぽいもの（揚げ物、チーズ、マヨネーズなど）

❹ 歯ごたえのあるもの（豆、ごま、漬物、オリーブなど）

❺ 薬味的なもの（大葉、生姜、フライドオニオンなど）

❻ 彩りのきれいなもの（紅しょうが、青のり、黒こしょう、黒ご

Many people ask, what kinds of fillings are best for making onigiri? My answer is always the same—anything that goes well with rice.

We can breakdown the fillings into the following categories:

❶ Sour（salt, soy sauce, miso, chile pepper etc.）

❷ Sweet（sauce, sweet cooked vegetables, dried fruits etc.）

❸ Rich with oil（deep-fried dishes, cheese, mayonnaise etc.）

❹ Rich in texture（beans, sesame, pickles, olives etc.）

まなど）

パラパラとまとまりにくい具には、味噌系、マヨネーズなどをまぜてまとめやすくするなど、味の相性以外に素材の性質も考えるとよいでしょう。

❶〜❻のグループのうち2つ、3つの組み合わせを考え、和風にするか、洋風にするか、または和洋のミックスにするか……とイメージを膨らませていくのもいいかと思います。オリジナルの具材を考えるのも楽しいでしょう。

❺ Flavorful（ooba, ginger, fried onion flakes etc.）
❻ Colorful（beni shoga, aonori, black pepper, black sesame etc.）
Try mixing miso or mayonnaise into fillings that are crumbly and hard to bind. This will make the onigiri making process easier. Experiment with different condiments depending on the filling.
Use the list above to consider various combinations and have fun creating your original fillings!

のりの使い方

おにぎりにのりはつきものですが、のりをいつ巻くかで食感がまったく違います。にぎってすぐにのりを巻くと、しっとりとご飯になじみ、食べるときはご飯との一体感を味わえます。食べる直前にのりを巻くと、のりのパリパリとした香ばしさを楽しめます。いつ巻くかはお好みでお楽しみいただき、ここではのりの基本の切り方と巻き方を紹介します。

The texture of an onigiri can be controlled by how long you wait before wrapping it in nori. Immediately wrapping a fresh onigiri will make the nori cling to the rice, and one can enjoy a harmonious, moist texture. However, if you prefer the crispiness of the nori, we recommend wrapping it right before eating the onigiri. Time the wrapping according to your preference. In this chapter, we will go over how to cut and wrap nori.

21 cm

19cm

のりのサイズ Size of Nori

のりの基本サイズは、縦21cm×横19cm。縦方向、横方向で切るかでサイズが少し変わります。

The standard size of a sheet of nori is 21 cm ×19 cm. You can change the size of the nori by cutting lengthwise or widthwise.

のりを切る Cutting Nori

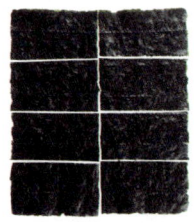

半切り Half

8つ切り Eighths

3つ切り Thirds

のりを巻く Wrapping Nori

すっぽりと全部を
包みたいときに。

Best for covering the
entire onigiri.

小さな俵形や軍艦
巻きのときに。

Best for small tawara
shapes and gunkan-style
onigiri.

三角形のおにぎり
などに。

Best for triangular onigiri.

のりで遊ぶ Have Fun with Nori!

おにぎりにのりを付けたキャラ弁は子どもたちにも人気です。
キャラ弁用に切られたのりも売っていますが、はさみで切って、
オリジナルのキャラ弁にも挑戦してみてください。

Children love creative bentos—especially ones with cute characters and animals.
Pre-cut nori for such "character bentos" can be found in stores, but why not pick
up a pair of scissors and take up "nori art" to make your original character bento?
Have fun!

この本の使い方

- ご飯の分量は、三角おにぎり1個でご飯約100g、俵おにぎりで50gを目安にしています。
- ご飯は基本、炊きたてを使います。
- おにぎりをにぎるときは、手水（手に水をつけて湿らせる）をつけ、塩少々を両手になじませるようにしてにぎると、ご飯が手にくっつきません。
- すべてのおにぎりをにぎるときに塩を使っていますので、材料に明記していません。
- 塩の加減は、中にいれる具材の塩分を考えましょう。にぎりたてを食べるときは軽く、お弁当など時間がたってからたべるときは強めが基本です。
- レシピは、炊き込みご飯おにぎり（p.118参照）以外はおにぎり1個分の材料です。
- 炊き込みご飯の米1合で、おにぎり約3個分ができます。
- 調理の必要なおかず具材の作り方は「おかずレシピ」（p.172〜）にのせています。
- 小さじ1＝5cc、大さじ1＝15cc、1カップ＝200ccを使用しています。

- All recipes make a single triangular onigiri using 100 grams of rice or a tawara (cylinder-shaped) onigiri using 50 grams of rice.
- Always use freshly cooked rice.
- Before making an onigiri, lightly wet your hands with water and sprinkle a pinch of salt on your palms. This will prevent the rice from sticking to your fingers.
- Salt is not listed in the ingredients. Adjust the amount of salt to your preference, taking into account the saltiness of the fillings and when the onigiri will be consumed. More salt will preserve the onigiri for a longer period of time.
- All recipes yield a single onigiri except for the Takikomi-Gohan (see p.118) which yields 3 onigiri.
- Onigiri fillings that need to be cooked are introduced in the "Okazu Recipe" chapter (see p.172).
- Refer to the ingredient glossary (see p.192) for information on ingredients.
- In this book, we use these standard measurements: 1 tsp=5 ml, 1 tbsp=15 ml, 1 cup=200 ml (These are standard Japanese conversions.)

1. 中に入れる

FILL

具材を中に入れてにぎる

HOW TO FILL ONIGIRI

おにぎりの基本形は、真ん中に具を入れてにぎります。初心者の方には、お茶碗にご飯を入れ、真ん中に具材をおき、それから手に移してにぎることをおすすめしますが、ここでは基本的な手順を紹介します。

A classic onigiri is made by filling the center of a handful of rice with ingredients. For beginners, fill a small rice bowl with rice and place the filling in the center. Then, transfer the rice into the hands and mold it into an onigiri. Here, we will go over the basics of how to make an onigiri with fillings.

❶ 手水をつけ、塩をつけた手にご飯をのせ、軽くにぎります。

Lightly wet your hands with water and sprinkle a pinch of salt on your palms. Place some rice in your palm and gently, but firmly, cup the rice.

❷ ご飯の真ん中にくぼみをつくっておきます。

Make a dent in the center of the rice.

❸ くぼみに具材を入れます。

Place the filling in the dent.

❹ 中に入れた具材を包み込むようににぎります。

Fold the rice over the dent and cover the filling by molding the rice with both hands.

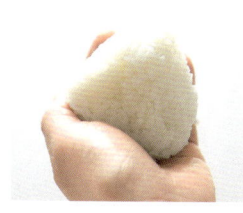

❺ 三角形や俵など、好きな形ににぎって出来上がりです。のりを巻いたり、ごまをふったりと後はお好みで。

Mold the rice into a triangle, tawara (cylinder-shaped), or any shape you prefer and you have an onigiri. Sprinkle sesame or wrap with nori according to your preference.

001 ツナマヨ・高菜

Tuna Mayo & Takana

[材料]

ツナ缶…15g、マヨネーズ…小1、高菜の漬け物…10g

❶ 高菜は細かく刻む。

❷ ツナ、マヨネーズ、高菜をまぜ、ご飯の真ん中に入れて、好きな形ににぎる。

• 15 grams canned tuna
• 1 tsp mayonnaise
• 10 grams takanazuke, finely chopped

❶ In a bowl, mix all the ingredients together.

❷ Scoop one serving of rice into your hand and place ❶ in the center. Mold the rice into an onigiri of your preferred shape.

梅干し・クリームチーズ
Umeboshi & Cream Cheese

［材料］
梅干し…1個、クリームチーズ…キューブ1個
❶ 梅干しの種をとり、ほぐす。
❷ クリームチーズはキューブの形のまま、梅干しにそえるようにして、ご飯の真ん中に入れ、好きな形ににぎる。

• 1 umeboshi, pitted and mashed
• 1 cm cube cream cheese
❶ Scoop one serving of rice into your hand and place the umeboshi and cream cheese in the center. Mold the rice into an onigiri of your preferred shape.

003 めんたいこ・たらこ

Mentaiko & Tarako

[材料]

めんたいこ…20g、たらこ…20g

❶ めんたいことたらこを同量にするのがポイント。

❷ まぜ合わせずに、ご飯の真ん中に入れて、好きな形ににぎる。

• 20 grams mentaiko
• 20 grams tarako

❶ The key is to have equal amounts of mentaiko and tarako.

❷ Scoop one serving of rice into your hand and place the mentaiko and tarako in the center. Mold the rice into an onigiri of your preferred shape.

004 焼き鳥

Yakitori

［材料］

鶏肉（もも、胸どちらでも）…サイコロ状で3個、酒…小2、醤油…小1/2、
砂糖…小1/2、みりん…小1/2、サラダ油…小1/2

❶ フライパンにサラダ油をひいて、鶏肉を軽く焼いてから調味料で味をととのえる。

❷ ご飯の真ん中に❶を入れて、好きな形ににぎる。

• 1/2 tsp cooking oil, for the pan • 3 diced pieces chicken breast or thigh
• 2 tsp sake • 1/2 tsp soy sauce • 1/2 tsp sugar • 1/2 tsp mirin

❶ Heat the oil in a pan over medium heat and cook the chicken pieces until nicely
browned. Season the chicken with sake, soy sauce, sugar, and mirin and adjust to
taste.

❷ Scoop one serving of rice into your hand and place ❶ in the center. Mold the
rice into an onigiri of your preferred shape.

005 ゆかり・サツマイモ

Yukari & Sweet Potato

[材料]

ゆかり… 大1、サツマイモ…15g

❶ サツマイモは皮を剥いて、2㎝ほどの大きさに切ってから茹でる。

❷ ご飯にゆかりをまぶして軽くまぜ合わせておく。ご飯の真ん中に❶を入れて、好きな形ににぎる。

• 15 grams sweet potato, peeled and diced into 2 cm pieces
• 1 tbsp yukari

❶ Boil the sweet potato in water until soft.
❷ In a bowl, mix the yukari and rice.
❸ Scoop one serving of rice into your hand and place ❶ in the center. Mold the rice into an onigiri of your preferred shape.

006 麻婆豆腐

Mapo Tofu

[材料]
麻婆豆腐…小2
❶ 麻婆豆腐のつくり方はp.172を参照。
❷ 麻婆豆腐の汁気をよく切り、ご飯の真ん中に入れて、好きな形ににぎる。

• 2 tsp mapo tofu
❶ See p.172 for mapo tofu recipe.
❷ Scoop one serving of rice into your hand and place the mapo tofu in the center.
Mold the rice into an onigiri of your preferred shape.

007 ホタテ味噌

Scallop Miso

[材料]
ホタテ…1個、味噌…小1、酒…小1/2、みりん…小1/2、バター…小1/2

❶ ホタテをサイコロ状に切る。

❷ 味噌に酒とみりんを入れてまぜる。

❸ フライパンにバターをひいてホタテを焼き、焼き色がついたら❷をいれ、汁気がなくなるまで焼く。

❹ ご飯の真ん中に❸を入れて、好きな形ににぎる。

• 1/2 tsp sake   • 1/2 tsp mirin   • 1 tsp miso
• 1/2 tsp butter, for the pan   • 1 scallop, diced into small cubes

❶ In a bowl, mix the sake, mirin, and miso.

❷ Heat the butter in a pan and sauté the scallops until nicely browned. Gently pour ❶ into the pan and stir until caramelized.

❸ Scoop one serving of rice into your hand and place ❷ in the center. Mold the rice into an onigiri of your preferred shape.

008 すき焼き

Sukiyaki

［材料］
すき焼き…大1、紅しょうが…小1/2
❶ すき焼きのつくり方はp.173を参照。
❷ すき焼きは汁気をよく切ってから、紅しょうがといっしょにご飯の真ん中に入れて、好きな形ににぎる。

• 1 tbsp sukiyaki　　• 1/2 tsp beni shoga
❶ See p.173 for sukiyaki recipe.Take a spoonful and squeeze out the excess liquid.
❷ Scoop one serving of rice into your hand and place the sukiyaki and beni shoga in the center. Mold the rice into an onigiri of your preferred shape.

009 アボカドわさび醤油

Avocado Wasabi Soy Sauce

[材料]

アボカド…1/4個、醤油…小1/2、わさび…小1/2

❶ アボカドをサイコロ状に切る。

❷ 醤油とわさびをまぜ、❶をあえる。

❸ ご飯の真ん中に❷を入れて、好きな形ににぎる。

• 1/2 tsp soy sauce　　• 1/2 tsp wasabi　　• 1/4 avocado, diced

❶ In a bowl, mix the soy sauce and wasabi. Add the avocado and mix well.

❷ Scoop one serving of rice into your hand and place ❶ in the center. Mold the rice into an onigiri of your preferred shape.

010 から揚げ

Karaage（Deep-Fried Chicken）

［材料］

鶏のから揚げ…1つ

❶ から揚げのつくり方はp.174を参照。

❷ 小さめのから揚げが入れやすいが、大きいものはご飯からはみだして見えるようににぎる。

• 1 piece karaage（deep-fried chicken）

❶ See p.174 for karaage recipe.

❷ Scoop one serving of rice into your hand and place the karaage in the center. Mold the rice into an onigiri of your preferred shape. A small piece of karaage is preferable, but when using a large piece, let it peek out of the onigiri.

011 黒豆・パルメジャンチーズ

Black Beans & Parmesan Cheese

［材料］
黒豆煮…5粒、パルメジャンチーズ…大1/2
❶ 黒豆煮のつくり方はp.175を参照。
❷ パルメジャンチーズをすりおろし、ご飯に軽くまぜ合わせる。
❸ 黒豆をご飯の真ん中に入れて、パルメジャンチーズを少し振りかけ、好きな形ににぎる。

• 5 black beans, sweet simmered   • 1/2 tbsp freshly grated parmesan cheese
❶ See p.175 for sweet simmered black beans. In a bowl, mix the parmesan cheese and rice.
❷ Scoop one serving of rice into your hand and place the black beans in the center. Mold the rice into an onigiri of your preferred shape.

012 納豆・柴漬け・たくあん

Natto, Shibazuke & Takuan

[材料]

納豆…大1/2、柴漬け…小1、たくあん…小1

❶ 柴漬けとたくあんは細かく刻む。

❷ 納豆と❶をよくまぜ合わせ、ご飯の真ん中に入れて、好きな形ににぎる。

• 1 tsp shibazuke pickles, finely chopped

• 1 tsp takuan pickles, finely chopped

• 1/2 tbsp natto

❶ In a bowl, mix the shibazuke pickles, takuan pickles, and natto.

❷ Scoop one serving of rice into your hand and place ❶ in the center. Mold the rice into an onigiri of your preferred shape.

013 こんにゃく甘辛煮・ごま

Sweet-and-Salty Konnyaku & Sesame

[材料]
こんにゃく甘辛煮…大1、ごま…小1
❶ こんにゃく甘辛煮のつくり方はp.176を参照。
❷ 汁気を切った❶にごまをまぶして、ご飯の真ん中に入れてにぎる。

• 1 tbsp sweet-and-salty simmered konnyaku, drained
• 1 tsp sesame
❶ See p.176 for sweet-and-salty konnyaku recipe.
❷ Sprinkle sesame on top of the konnyaku.
❸ Scoop one serving of rice into your hand and place ❷ in the center. Mold the rice into an onigiri of your preferred shape.

014 トマトご飯・ソーセージ

Tomato Rice & Sausage

[材料]

ケチャップ…大1、ウインナーソーセージ…1本、サラダ油…少々

❶ フライパンにサラダ油をひいて、おにぎり1個分のご飯を炒め、ケチャップを入れ、トマトご飯をつくる。

❷ ウインナーソーセージは長さの半分のところまで、4等分に切り込みを入れて、フライパンで焼く。

❸ 切り込み部分がおにぎりから出るようにしてにぎる。

- • 1/2 tsp cooking oil, for the pan
- • 1 tbsp ketchup
- • 1 sausage, cut into a little octopus (see below) along the sides

❶ Heat the oil in a pan over medium heat. Add the rice and ketchup and stir-fry the rice.

❷ Using a sharp knife, slice the sausage in half lengthwise, leaving an inch connected at one end. Roll the sausage 90 degrees and repeat.

❸ Heat a pan over medium heat and cook the sausage until browned.

❹ Scoop one serving of ❶ into your hand, and place ❸ in the center so the cut-end of the sausage faces up. Mold the rice into an onigiri of your preferred shape. Let the sausage peek out of the onigiri.

015 きんぴら

Kinpira

[材料]

きんぴら…大1

❶ きんぴらのつくり方はp.176を参照。

❷ きんぴらを食べやすいように短めに切り、ご飯の真ん中に入れてにぎる。

• 1 tbsp kinpira, cut into short pieces
❶ See p.176 for kinpira recipe.
❷ Scoop one serving of rice into your hand and place the kinpira in the center.
Mold the rice into an onigiri of your preferred shape.

016 押し麦ご飯・サワークリーム・たらこ

Rolled Barley & Tarako with Sour Cream

[材料]
押し麦…1袋（p.203参照）、米…2合、サワークリーム…小2、たらこ…小2
❶ 米2合に押し麦1本を入れて基本のご飯の炊き方で炊く（p.12参照）。
❷ サワークリームとたらこをよくまぜる。
❸ ❷の具材をおにぎり1個分の❶の真ん中に入れて、好きな形ににぎる。

• 1 pack rolled barley（see p.203）   • 2 cups of rice
• 2 tsp sour cream   • 2 tsp tarako
❶ Wash 2 cups of rice and add 2 cups of water. Add a pack of Rolled Barley to the rice and water and cook the rice（see p.12）.
❷ In a bowl, mix the sour cream and cod roe.
❸ Scoop one serving of rice into your hand and place ❷ in the center. Mold the rice into an onigiri of your preferred shape.

017 おかかマヨ

Okaka & Mayo

[材料]

おかか…1/3袋（1g）、マヨネーズ…小1/2、醤油…小1/4

❶ おかかにマヨネーズと醤油をまぜ合わせる。

❷ ご飯の真ん中に❶を入れて、好きな形ににぎる。

- 1/2 tsp mayonnaise
- 1/4 tsp soy sauce
- 1 gram or 1/3 pack okaka

❶ In a bowl, mix the mayonnaise, soy sauce, and okaka.

❷ Scoop one serving of rice into your hand and place ❶ in the center. Mold the rice into an onigiri of your preferred shape.

018 鮭・いくら

［材料］
生鮭…1/4切れ、いくら…小2、塩…少々
❶ 生鮭は軽く塩をふり、グリルで焼く。フライパンで焼く場合は、薄くサラ
ダ油をひき、強火で皮目からしっかり焼き、裏返して弱火でじっくり焼く。
❷ 焼いた鮭はほぐしておく。鮭にイクラをそえ、ご飯の中に入れて、いくら
をつぶさないようににぎる。

• 25 grams salmon, lightly salted　　• 1/4 tsp salt　　• 2 tsp ikura
❶ Grill the salmon on a grill. If using a pan, heat some oil over high heat and place
the salmon skin-side down and cook. Flip over the salmon, turn down the heat and
cook slowly until the salmon is completely cooked.
❷ Break the salmon into flakes. Scoop one serving of rice into your hand, and
place the salmon and ikura in the center. Carefully mold the rice into an onigiri.
Try to avoid crushing the ikura.

019 ウスター卵

Worcestershire Egg

［材料］

卵…1個、ウスターソース…1/2カップ、
酢… 1/2カップ、黒ごま…小1

❶ 卵を茹でて、同量のウスターソースと酢にひと晩漬ける。

❷ ご飯でつつむようにして❶をにぎる。 おにぎりのまわりにごまをまぶす。

• 1/2 cup Worcestershire sauce
• 1/2 cup vinegar　　• 1 egg, boiled
• 1 tsp black sesame

❶ In a bowl, mix the Worcestershire sauce and vinegar. Soak the boiled egg in the mixture overnight.
❷ Scoop one serving of rice into your hand and place ❶ in the center. Mold it into an onigiri of your preferred shape. Sprinkle sesame on the outside.

020 しゅうまい

Shumai Dumpling

［材料］

しゅうまい…1個、醤油…小1、練り辛子…小1/2

❶ しゅうまいのつくり方はp.177を参照。 小ぶりのしゅうまいにする。

❷ 醤油に練り辛子を溶き、❶にからめ、ご飯の真ん中に入れてにぎる。

• 1 tsp soy sauce　　• 1/2 tsp karashi paste
• 1 shumai dumpling

❶ See p.177 for shumai dumpling recipe. Small ones are preferred.
❷ In a bowl, mix the soy sauce and karashi paste. Pour the mixture on the shumai dumpling.
❸ Scoop one serving of rice into your hand and place ❷ in the center. Mold it into an onigiri of your preferred shape.

021 まぐろ漬け

Maguro Zuke

[材料]

まぐろの刺身…1切れ、醤油…小1、わさび…少々

❶ まぐろを小ぶりのサイコロ状に切る。

❷ 醤油とわさびをまぜ合わせ、❶を10分漬ける。

❸ ❷の汁気を切って、ご飯の真ん中に入れ、好きな形ににぎる。

• 1 tsp soy sauce   • 1/4 tsp wasabi
• 1 slice maguro sashimi, diced into small cubes

❶ In a bowl, mix the soy sauce and wasabi and soak the sashimi for 10 minutes. Drain the excess liquid.

❷ Scoop one serving of rice into your hand and place ❶ in the center. Mold it into an onigiri of your preferred shape.

022 味噌梅

Umeboshi & Miso

[材料]
梅干し…1個、味噌…小1、砂糖…小1、すりごま…小1、おかか…適宜
❶ 梅干しの種をとり細かく叩いて、味噌と砂糖で味をととのえ、すりゴマと
おかかをまぜ合わせる。
❷ ご飯の真ん中に❶を入れて、好きな形ににぎる。

• 1 umeboshi, pitted and minced　　• 1 tsp miso　　• 1 tsp sugar
• 1 tsp ground sesame　　• 1 tsp okaka
❶ In a bowl, mix the umeboshi, miso, sugar, and sesame. Add the okaka to taste.
❷ Scoop one serving of rice into your hand and place ❶ in the center. Mold it into
an onigiri of your preferred shape.

023 えのき辛煮

Salty Sautéed Enoki

[材料]
えのき…15g、酒…大1、醤油…大1
❶ えのきは半分に切る。
❷ 鍋に❶と酒と醤油を入れて、水気がなくなるまで煮る。
❸ ご飯の真ん中に❷を入れて、好きな形ににぎる。

• 15 grams enoki, cut into half
• 1 tbsp sake
• 1 tbsp soy sauce
❶ In a pot over medium heat, add the enoki, sake, and soy sauce. Simmer until the liquid is reduced.
❷ Scoop one serving of rice into your hand and place ❶ in the center. Mold the rice into an onigiri of your preferred shape.

024 粒マスタード鮭

Grain Mustard Salmon

［材料］

生鮭…1/4切れ、粒マスタード…大1/2、塩…少々

❶ 生鮭は軽く塩をふり、グリルで焼く。フライパンで焼く場合は、薄くサラ
ダ油をひき、強火で皮目からしっかり焼き、裏返して弱火でじっくり焼く。

❷ 焼いた鮭をほぐし、粒マスタードであえる。

❸ ご飯の真ん中に❷を入れて、好きな形ににぎる。

• 25 grams salmon, lightly salted　　• 1/4 tsp salt　　• 1/2 tbsp grain mustard

❶ Grill the salmon on a grill. If using a pan, heat the oil over high heat and place
the salmon skin-side down and cook well. Flip over the salmon, turn down the heat
and cook slowly until the salmon is completely cooked.

❷ Break the salmon into flakes, and mix well with the grain mustard.

❸ Scoop one serving of rice into your hand and place ❷ in the center. Mold the
rice into an onigiri of your preferred shape.

025 ごま塩

Sesame Salt

［材料］

黒ごま…大1/2

❶ 基本のおにぎりより、やや強めに塩をきかせてにぎる。

❷ 黒ごまを❶にたっぷりとまぶす。

• 1/2 tbsp black sesame
• 1/2 tsp salt

❶ Apply the salt on your hands and mold an onigiri of your preferred shape.

❷ Generously cover the onigiri with black sesame.

2. まぜる
MIX

まぜてにぎる

HOW TO MAKE MIXED ONIGIRI

ご飯と具材をまぜ合わせてからにぎるおにぎりを紹介します。ご飯にまんべんなく味がいきわたるので、塩分、ソースなどは控えめにします。2、3種類の具材を組み合わせ、見た目の彩りをポイントとして考えるとよいでしょう。

A mixed onigiri is made by blending the filling with the rice before packing it into an onigiri. Use seasonings such as salt and sauce sparingly since the mixing process will distribute the flavor evenly. Mix and combine 2-3 different fillings for a colorful and beautiful onigiri.

❶ ボウルに具材を入れます。具材の量は、ご飯の量に対して多すぎないように注意しましょう。まとまりにくくなります。

Put the fillings into a bowl. Make sure the portion is appropriate for the amount of rice. It will be difficult to mold the onigiri with too much filling.

❷ まぜ合わせた具材にご飯を入れ、さらによくまぜ合わせます。

Add the rice and mix well.

❸ 両手に塩をつけて、まぜ合わせたご飯を手のひらにのせてにぎります。具材に味がついているときは、塩は控えめにしてにぎります。

Lightly wet your hands with water and sprinkle a pinch of salt on your palms. When using strong flavored fillings, use salt sparingly.

❹ 好きな形ににぎって出来上がりです。まとまりにくい具材の場合は、ラップを使ってにぎるとよいでしょう。

Place some rice in your palm, then firmly, but gently, cup and squeeze the rice using both hands. Mold it into an onigiri of your preferred shape. Depending on the filling, you may find it difficult to bind the onigiri. If this is the case, use saran wrap to wrap the rice.

026 三色おにぎり

Tricolor Onigiri

［材料］

丸おにぎり1個…ご飯40g、卵…1個、
青のり…小1、でんぶ…小1、すし酢…小2

❶ 卵は茹でて、黄身だけをざるなどで裏ごしする。

❷ ご飯に❶をよくまぜあわせ、ラップを使ってピンポン玉大ににぎる。

❸ 塩を少し多めに使ってご飯を軽くにぎり、ラップを使ってピンポン玉大ににぎり、青のりをまぶす。

❹ ご飯にすし酢をまぜて、ラップを使ってピンポン玉大ににぎる。

❺ でんぶを❹にまぶす。

This recipe makes 3 onigiri:
- 120 grams cooked rice
- 1 egg, boiled
- 1 tsp aonori
- 2 tsp sushi vinegar
- 1 tsp denbu

❶ Grate the boiled egg yolk with a sieve to turn it into powder form.

❷ In a bowl, mix ❶ and 40 grams of rice to make the first onigiri. Wrap it in saran wrap, and mold it into a ping pong-shaped ball. Take off the wrap and set aside.

❸ For the second onigiri, apply ample salt on your hands and make a ball using 40 grams of rice. Wrap it in saran wrap and mold it into a ping pong-shaped ball. Take off the wrap and sprinkle aonori on the outside.

❹ For the third onigiri, in a bowl, mix the sushi vinegar and 40 grams of rice. Wrap it in saran wrap and mold it into a ping pong-shaped ball. Take off the wrap and sprinkle denbu on the outside.

グリーンオリーブ ・ オリーブのり

Green Olive & Olive Nori

［材料］

グリーンオリーブ（種なし）…3個、黒こしょう…少々、

オリーブのり…1枚（p.203参照）

❶ グリーンオリーブを細かく刻む。

❷ ご飯に❶をまぜ合わせ、黒こしょうを全体にふり、俵形おにぎりをにぎる。

❸ おにぎりにオリーブのりを巻く。

• 3 green olives, pitted and finely chopped
• 1/4 tsp black pepper
• 1 olive nori（see p.203）

❶ In a bowl, mix the olives and rice and black pepper.

❷ Scoop ❶ into your hand and mold it into a tawara (cylinder-shaped) onigiri.

❸ Wrap ❷ with olive nori.

028 アンチョビ・サラミ（芽ぐみ米）

Anchovy Salami（with Megumimai）

［材料］
芽ぐみ米…1個分（p.203参照）、アンチョビ…小1/2、サラミ…小1、
イタリアンパセリ…小2
❶ 芽ぐみ米を基本のご飯の炊き方で炊く（p.12参照）。
❷ アンチョビ、サラミ、イタリアンパセリを細かく切り、軽くまぜ合わせる。
❸ おにぎり1個分の芽ぐみ米と❷をまぜ合わせて、好きな形ににぎる。

• 50 grams Megumimai, cooked（see p.203）
• 1/2 tsp finely chopped anchovy
• 1 tsp finely chopped salami
• 2 tsp finely chopped Italian parsley
❶ Cook the rice using Megumimai（see p.12）.
❷ In a bowl, mix the anchovy, salami, and parsley. Mix well with ❶.
❸ Scoop one serving of ❷ into your hand and mold it into an onigiri of your
preferred shape.

029 枝豆・塩昆布

Edamame & Shiokombu

[材料]

枝豆（茹でたもの）…10粒、塩昆布…2つまみ

❶ 枝豆と塩昆布をまぜ合わせる。

❷ ご飯と❶をまぜて、好きな形ににぎる。

• 10 edamame beans, boiled in the pods and shelled
• 2 pinches shiokombu
❶ In a bowl, mix the edamame, shiokombu, and rice.
❷ Scoop ❶ into your hand and mold it into an onigiri of your preferred shape.

030 新しょうが・大葉・ごま

Pickled Spring Ginger, Ooba & Sesame

[材料]
新しょうがの甘酢漬け…小1、大葉…1枚、ごま…小1/2
❶ 新しょうがの甘酢漬けのつくり方はp.178を参照。
❷ 新しょうがと大葉は細かく刻む。
❸ ごまと❷をご飯とまぜ合わせ、好きな形ににぎる。

• 1 tsp pickled spring ginger, finely chopped
• 1 ooba, finely chopped
• 1/2 tsp sesame
❶ See p.178 for pickled spring ginger recipe.
❷ In a bowl, mix the pickled spring ginger, sesame, and rice.
❸ Scoop ❶ into your hand and mold it into an onigiri of your preferred shape.

031 焼きたらこ

［材料］
たらこ…1/2腹、サラダ油…小1/2
❶ たらこはグリルで焼くか、フライパンに薄くサラダ油をひいて焼く。
❷ ❶をほぐして、ご飯にまぜ合わせて、好きな形ににぎる。

• 2 tbsp tarako
• 1/2 tsp cooking oil, for the pan
❶ Grill the tarako over a grill. If using a pan, heat the oil over medium heat and cook the tarako until it turns light pink and firm.
❷ Break the tarako apart and mix well with the rice.
❸ Scoop ❷ into your hand and mold it into an onigiri of your preferred shape.

032 おかか・ごま

Okaka & Sesame

[材料]

おかか…1袋（3g）、醤油…小1、ごま…小1/2

❶ おかかに醤油を合わせる。

❷ ご飯に❶をまぜ合わせ、最後にごまをいれて軽くまぜて、好きな形ににぎる。

- 1 tsp soy sauce
- 1 pack or 3 grams okaka
- 1/2 tsp sesame

❶ In a bowl, mix the soy sauce and okaka. Add the rice, and mix in the sesame last.

❷ Scoop ❶ into your hand and mold it into an onigiri of your preferred shape.

033 わかめ・カニカマ

Wakame Seaweed & Kanikama

[材料]

わかめ（戻したもの）…15g、カニカマ…1本、

醤油…少々、ごま油…小1/2

❶ 戻したわかめを細かく刻み、フライパンにごま油をひいて醤油で炒める。

❷ カニカマは細かく刻む。

❸ ご飯に❶と❷をまぜ合わせて、好きな形ににぎる。

• 15 grams wakame seaweed, rehydrated and finely chopped
• 1 stick kanikama, finely chopped   • a drizzle of soy sauce
• 1/2 tsp sesame oil, for the pan

❶ Heat the sesame oil in a pan over medium heat. Drizzle the wakame with soy sauce and sauté.

❷ In a bowl, mix the kanikama and ❶ into the rice.

❸ Scoop ❷ into your hand and mold it into an onigiri of your preferred shape.

034 長芋・オクラ

Chinese Yam & Okra

[材料]

長芋…1㎝、オクラ…2本

❶ オクラはさっと塩ゆでして、5㎜幅の輪切りにする。

❷ 長芋は5㎜角に切る。

❸ ご飯に❶と❷をまぜて、好きな形ににぎる。

• 1 cm Chinese yam, diced into 5 mm pieces
• 2 okras, lightly boiled in salt water and sliced into 5 mm pieces
❶ In a bowl, mix the yam, okras, and rice.
❷ Scoop ❶ into your hand and mold it into an onigiri of your preferred shape.

035 もち麦・梅干し

Waxy Barley & Umeboshi

[材料]
もち麦…1袋（p.203参照）、米…2合、梅干し…1個
❶ 米2合にもち麦1本を入れて基本のご飯の炊き方で炊く（p.12参照）。
❷ 種をとって細かく刻んだ梅干しを、おにぎり1個分の❶によくまぜて、好きな形ににぎる。

• 1 pack Waxy Barley（see p.203）
• 2 cups rice
• 1 umeboshi, pitted and minced
❶ Wash 2 cups of regular rice and add 2 cups of water. Add a pack of Waxy Barley and cook the rice（see p.12）.
❷ In a bowl, mix the umeboshi into one serving of ❶.
❸ Scoop ❷ into your hand and mold it into an onigiri of your preferred shape.

036 とうもろこし

Corn

［材料］
コーン（缶詰）…大2、
バター…小1
❶ フライパンにバターを入れて、汁気を切ったコーンを炒める。
❷ ご飯に❶をまぜ合わせ、好きな形ににぎる。

• 1 tsp butter, for the pan
• 2 tbsp canned corn, drained
❶ Heat the butter in a pan over medium heat. Stir-fry the corn and mix with rice.
❷ Scoop ❶ into your hand and mold it into an onigiri of your preferred shape.

037 カリカリ梅・大葉・ごま

Kari Kari Ume, Ooba & Sesame

［材料］
カリカリ梅…3個、大葉…2枚、
ごま…小1/2
❶ カリカリ梅は種をとって細かく刻
み、大葉はせん切りにする。
❷ ご飯に❶とごまをまぜ合わせて、
好きな形ににぎる。

• 3 kari kari ume, finely chopped
• 2 ooba, julienned
• 1/2 tsp sesame
❶ In a bowl, mix the kari kari ume, ooba, sesame, and rice.
❷ Scoop ❶ into your hand and mold it into an onigiri of your preferred shape.

038 ブロッコリースプラウト・じゃこ・ごま

Broccoli Sprout, Jyako & Sesame

[材料]
ブロッコリースーパースプラウト…大1（p.203参照）、
じゃこ…小1、ごま…小1/2
❶ ブロッコリースーパースプラウトを1㎝程度の長さに切る。
❷ ご飯に❶とじゃこ、ごまをまぜ合わせて、好きな形ににぎる。

• 1 tbsp broccoli super sprout, cut into 1 cm pieces（see p.203）
• 1 tsp jyako
• 1/2 tsp sesame
❶ In a bowl, mix the broccoli super sprout, jyako, sesame, and rice.
❷ Scoop ❶ into your hand and mold it into an onigiri of your preferred shape.

039 油揚げ・柚子こしょう

Deep-Fried Tofu & Yuzukosho

［材料］

油揚げ…1/3枚、醤油…小1、柚子こしょう…小1/2

❶ 油揚げは細かく刻み、フライパンでから炒りし、醤油、柚子こしょうで味
をつける。

❷ ご飯に❶をまぜ合わせて、好きな形ににぎる。

• 1/3 deep-fried tofu, finely chopped
• 1 tsp soy sauce
• 1/2 tsp yuzukosho

❶ Heat a pan over medium heat and stir-fry the deep-fried tofu until lightlly browned. Add the soy sauce and yuzukosho to taste. Mix the deep-fried tofu with the rice.

❷ Scoop ❶ into your hand and mold it into an onigiri of your preferred shape.

040 ドライトマト・クリームチーズ・ケッパー

Sun-Dried Tomato, Cream Cheese & Caper

[材料]

ドライトマト…1かけ、クリームチーズ…5mm角を4個、ケッパー…小1

❶ ドライトマトは細かく刻む。

❷ ケッパーと❶をご飯とまぜ合わせ、最後にクリームチーズを入れ、軽くまぜ、好きな形ににぎる。

• 1 sun-dried tomato, finely chopped
• 1 tsp caper
• 4 dices cream cheese, 5 mm cubes
❶ In a bowl, mix the dried tomato, caper, and rice.
❷ Mix the cream cheese with ❶ gently.
❸ Scoop ❷ into your hand and mold it into an onigiri of your preferred shape.

041 そば飯
Yakisoba Rice

[材料]
焼きそば…50g、ご飯…50g、サラダ油…小1/2
❶ 焼きそばのつくり方はp.178を参照。焼きそばは1㎝程度の長さに切る。
❷ フライパンにサラダ油を薄くひいて、❶とご飯を入れて炒める。
❸ 少し冷ましてから、好きな形ににぎる。

• 1/2 tsp cooking oil, for the pan
• 50 grams yakisoba, chopped into 1 cm pieces
• 50 grams rice
❶ See p.178 for yakisoba recipe.
❷ Heat the oil in a pan over medium heat. Add the rice and chopped yakisoba and stir until well mixed.
❸ When the yakisoba rice cools down, scoop it into your hand and mold it into an onigiri of your preferred shape.

042 16穀米・ピーマン・セロリ

16 Grains, Green Pepper & Celery

［材料］
16穀米…1袋（p.203参照）、米…2合、
ピーマン…1/2個、セロリ…2㎝

❶ 米2合に16穀米1袋を入れ、基本のご飯の炊き方で炊く
（p.12参照）。

❷ ピーマン、セロリはみじん切りにする。

❸ おにぎり1個分の❶に❷をまぜ合わせて、好きな形ににぎる。

• 1 pack 16 Grains, cooked（see p.203） • 2 cups rice
• 1/2 green pepper, minced • 2 cm celery, minced

❶ Wash 2 cups of regular rice and add 2 cups of water. Add a pack of 16 Grains and cook the rice（see p.12）.

❷ Add the green pepper and celery into one serving of ❶ and mix well.

❸ Scoop ❷ into your hand and mold it into an onigiri of your preferred shape.

043 キャロット

Carrot

[材料]
人参…10g、
ドレッシング（オリーブオイル…小1/2、レモン汁…小1/2、
塩…ひとつまみ、砂糖…ひとつまみ）
❶ ドレッシングの材料をよくまぜ合わせる。
❷ 人参は細いせん切りにして❶で和え、キャロットラペをつくる。
❸ ご飯に❷をまぜ合わせて、好きな形にぎる。

• 10 grams carrot, julienned
• dressing: 1/2 tsp olive oil, 1/2 tsp lemon juice, a pinch of salt,
a pinch of sugar
❶ In a bowl, mix the olive oil, lemon juice, salt, and sugar.
❷ Dress the carrot with ❶ and mix with the rice.
❸ Scoop ❷ into your hand and mold it into an onigiri of your preferred
shape.

044 ミモレットチーズ

Mimolette Cheese

[材料]
ミモレットチーズ…大1
❶ ミモレットチーズをすりおろす。
❷ ご飯に❶をまぜ合わせて、好きな形ににぎる。

• 1 tbsp fresh mimolette cheese, grated
❶ In a bowl, mix the mimolette cheese and rice.
❷ Scoop ❶ into your hand and mold it into an onigiri of your preferred shape.

045 ザーサイ・数の子

Zha Cai & Kazunoko

[材料]
ザーサイ…10g、数の子…10g、ごま油…小1/2、ごま…小1/2
❶ 数の子は細かく切り、ザーサイはせん切りにする。
❷ ごま油とごまを合わせ、そこに❶をまぜる
❸ ご飯に❷をまぜ合わせて、好きな形ににぎる。

• 1/2 tsp sesame oil　　• 1/2 tsp sesame
• 10 grams zha cai, julienned　　• 10 grams kazunoko, chopped
❶ In a bowl, mix the sesame oil and sesame.
❷ Add the zha cai and kazunoko into ❶. Mix everything into the rice.
❸ Scoop ❷ into your hand and mold it into an onigiri of your preferred shape.

046 コリアンダー ・ スイートチリソース

Coriander & Sweet Chili Sauce

［材料］
コリアンダー…1本、
スイートチリソース…小2
❶ コリアンダーは1cmほどの長さに切る。
❷ ご飯にスイートチリソースと❶をまぜ
合わせて、好きな形ににぎる。

- 1 tbsp fresh coriander, chopped into
  1 cm pieces
- 2 tsp sweet chili sauce
❶ Mix the coriander, sweet chili sauce, and
rice.
❷ Scoop ❶ into your hand and mold it into
an onigiri of your preferred shape.

047 紅しょうが・青のり

Beni Shoga & Aonori

[材料]
紅しょうが…小1、青のり…小1弱
❶ 紅しょうがは細かく刻む。
❷ ご飯に❶をいれ、最後に青のりをまぜ合わせて、好きな形ににぎる。

• 1 tsp beni shoga, finely chopped
• 1 tsp aonori
❶ Mix the beni shoga, aonori, and rice.
❷ Scoop ❶ into your hand and mold it into an onigiri of your preferred shape.

048 豆苗

Pea Sprouts

[材料]
豆苗…大3（p.203参照）

❶ 豆苗は生のまま、細かく切る。

❷ ご飯に❶をまぜ合わせて、好きな形ににぎる。

• 3 tbsp finely chopped pea sprouts（see p.203）

❶ Mix the pea sprouts and rice.

❷ Scoop ❶ into your hand and mold it into an onigiri of your preferred shape.

049 アジの干物・ナンプラー

[材料]

アジの干物…30g、しょうが…小1、ナンプラー…小1/2

❶ アジの干物はグリルで香ばしく焼いてほぐす。

❷ しょうがはみじん切りにする。

❸ ナンプラーを❶に振り、しょうがのみじん切りとご飯にまぜ合わせて、好きな形ににぎる。

• 30 grams dried mackerel　　• 1/2 tsp fish sauce　　• 1 tsp ginger, minced

❶ Heat a pan over medium heat and grill the dried mackerel. Flake the meat from the bones.

❷ Pour the fish sauce on ❶ and add ginger. Mix with the rice.

❸ Scoop ❷ into your hand and mold it into an onigiri of your preferred shape.

050 ベーコン・コンテチーズ・松の実

Bacon, Comte Cheese & Pine Nuts

[材料]

ベーコン…1枚、コンテチーズ…10g、松の実…小1

❶ ベーコンは細かく切り、フライパンで弱火でカリッと炒める。

❷ 松の実はフライパンで軽く炒る。

❸ コンテチーズを1㎝角に切り、❶と❷にまぜる。

❹ ご飯に❸をまぜ合わせて、好きな形ににぎる。

• 1 slice bacon, finely chopped
• 10 grams comte cheese, cut into 1 cm pieces
• 1 tsp pine nuts

❶ Heat a pan over medium heat and cook the bacon until browned and crisp.
❷ Lightly roast the pine nuts in a pan over medium heat.
❸ In a bowl, mix ❶, ❷ and the cheese into the rice.
❹ Scoop ❸ into your hand and mold it into an onigiri of your preferred shape.

16穀米・枝豆

16 Grains & Edamame

[材料]
16穀米…1袋（p.203参照）、米…2合、枝豆（茹でたもの）…15粒

❶ 米2合に16穀米1袋を入れて基本のご飯の炊き方で炊く（p.12参照）。

❷ おにぎり1個分の❶に枝豆をまぜ合わせて、好きな形ににぎる。

• 1 pack 16 Grains（see p.203）　• 2 cups rice
• 15 edamame beans, boiled in the pods and shelled
❶ Wash 2 cups of regular rice and add 2 cups of water. Add a pack of 16 Grains and cook the rice（see p.12）.
❷ Add edamame into one serving of ❶ and mix well.
❸ Scoop ❷ into your hand and mold it into an onigiri of your preferred shape.

052 ミックスナッツ・レーズン

Mixed Nuts & Raisins

［材料］
ミックスナッツ…大1、レーズン…小1
❶ ミックスナッツは粗く刻む。
❷ ご飯に❶とレーズンをまぜ合わせて、好きな形ににぎる。

• 1 tbsp mixed nuts, coarsely chopped
• 1 tsp raisins
❶ In a bowl, mix the nuts and raisins and rice.
❷ Scoop ❶ into your hand and mold it into an onigiri of your preferred shape.

053 かぶの葉

[材料]

かぶの葉…1本、塩…小1/2

❶ かぶの葉は細かく刻み、塩でよく揉む。

❷ ❶がしんなりしたら、水で洗ってよく絞る。

❸ ご飯に❷を入れてまぜ合わせて、好きな形ににぎる。

• 2 tbsp turnip greens, finely chopped and rubbed with salt until soft
• 1/2 tsp salt

❶ Wash the chopped turnip. Drain the excess liquid and mix with the rice.

❷ Scoop ❶ into your hand and mold it into an onigiri of your preferred shape.

054 山形のだっし

Yamagata Dasshi

[材料]

だっし…大1

❶ だっしのつくり方はp.179を参照。

❷ だっしの汁気をよく切り、ご飯にまぜ合わせて、好きな形ににぎる。

• 1 tbsp dasshi

❶ See p.179 for dasshi recipe.

❷ Drain the excess liquid from the dasshi and mix with the rice.

❸ Scoop ❶ into your hand and mold it into an onigiri of your preferred shape.

055 チアーシード・えごまオイル

Chia Seed & Egoma Oil

[材料]
チアーシード…小1、えごまオイル…小1/2 （p.203参照）
❶ ご飯とチアーシードをまぜ合わせる。
❷ えごまオイルを❶にまぜ、好きな形ににぎる。

• 1 tsp chia seed
• 1/2 tsp egoma oil （see p.203）
❶ In a bowl, mix the chia seeds, egoma oil, and rice.
❷ Scoop ❶ into your hand and mold it into an onigiri of your preferred shape.

056 バジル・松の実

Basil & Pine Nuts

[材料]
バジルの葉…3枚、松の実…小1、黒こしょう…小1/2

❶ 松の実はフライパンで軽く炒る。
❷ バジルの葉は細かく刻む。
❸ ご飯に❶とバジルをまぜ合わせ、黒こしょうを振り、好きな形ににぎる。

- 1 tsp pine nuts
- 3 basil leaves, finely chopped
- 1/2 tsp black pepper

❶ Roast the pine nuts in a pan over medium heat.
❷ In a bowl, mix ❶, basil leaves, black pepper, and rice.
❸ Scoop ❷ into your hand and mold it into an onigiri of your preferred shape.

057 鮭フレーク

Salmon Flakes

[材料]
鮭フレーク（市販のもの）…大1、黒ごま…小1/2
❶ ご飯に鮭フレークを入れ、よくまぜる。
❷ 黒ごまを❶にまぜ合わせて、好きな形ににぎる。

• 1 tbsp store-bought salmon flakes
• 1/2 tsp black sesame
❶ In a bowl, mix the salmon flakes, black sesame, and rice.
❷ Scoop ❶ into your hand and mold it into an onigiri of your preferred shape.

058 たくあん

Takuan

[材料]
たくあん…10g、ごま…小1/2
❶ たくあんは薄く切ってからせん切りにする。
❷ ご飯に❶とごまをまぜ合わせて、好きな形ににぎる。

• 10 grams takuan, cut into thin slices, then julienned
• 1/2 tsp sesame
❶ In a bowl, mix the takuan, sesame, and rice.
❷ Scoop ❶ into your hand and mold it into an onigiri of your preferred shape.

059 ハム・パセリ

Ham & Parsley

[材料]

ハム…1枚、パセリ…大1

❶ ハムとパセリはみじん切りにする。

❷ ご飯に❶をまぜ合わせて、好きな形ににぎる。

• 1 slice ham, finely chopped
• 1 tbsp finely chopped parsley

❶ In a bowl, mix the ham, parsley, and rice.

❷ Scoop ❶ into your hand and mold it into an onigiri of your preferred shape.

060 ドライトマト・黒オリーブ
Sun-Dried Tomato & Black Olive

［材料］
ドライトマト…1かけ、黒オリーブ…6個
❶ ドライトマトはみじん切りにする。
❷ 黒オリーブは種をはずして、みじん切りにする。
❸ ご飯に❶と❷をまぜ合わせて、好きな形ににぎる。

• 1 sun-dried tomato, finely chopped
• 6 black olives, pitted and finely chopped
❶ In a bowl, mix the dried tomato, black olives, and rice.
❷ Scoop ❶ into your hand and mold it into an onigiri of your preferred shape.

061 あさりの佃煮

［材料］
あさりの佃煮…大1、しょうが…大1
❶ しょうがはみじん切りにする。
❷ ご飯にあさりの佃煮と❶を入れてまぜ合わせ、好きな形ににぎる。

• 1 tbsp tsukudai clam
• 1 tbsp minced ginger
❶ In a bowl, mix the tsukudani clam, ginger, and rice.
❷ Scoop ❶ into your hand and mold it into an onigiri of your preferred shape.

062 ひじき

Hijiki Seaweed

[材料]

ひじきの煮物…50g

❶ ひじきの煮物のつくり方はp.180を参照。

❷ ひじきの煮物は、汁気を切り、食べやすい大きさに切る。

❸ ご飯に❷をまぜ合わせて、好きな形ににぎる。

• 50 grams simmered hijiki seaweed, chopped

❶ See p.180 for simmered hijiki recipe. Drain the excess liquid of the hijiki.

❷ In a bowl, mix the hijiki seaweed and rice.

❸ Scoop ❷ into your hand and mold it into an onigiri of your preferred shape.

063 パルメジャンチーズ・生ハム

Parmesan Cheese & Prosciutto

[材料]

パルメジャンチーズ…小1、生ハム…1枚、黒こしょう…少々

❶ 生ハムは細かく切る。

❷ ご飯にパルメジャンチーズと黒こしょうを入れ、まぜる。

❸ ❷に❶をまぜ合わせて、好きな形ににぎる。

• 1 tsp parmesan cheese
• 1 slice prosciutto, finely chopped
• a pinch of black pepper
❶ In a bowl, mix the parmesan cheese, prosciutto, black pepper, and rice.
❷ Scoop ❶ into your hand and mold it into an onigiri of your preferred shape.

064 枝豆・コンテチーズ

Edamame & Comte Cheese

[材料]
枝豆（茹でたもの）…15粒、コンテチーズ…小1、醤油…小2
❶ コンテチーズを1cm角に切り、醤油にひたす。
❷ ご飯に枝豆と❶をまぜ合わせて、好きな形ににぎる。

• 1 tsp comte cheese, cut into 1 cm pieces
• 2 tsp soy sauce
• 15 edamame beans, boiled in the pods and shelled
❶ Soak the comte cheese in soy sauce.
❷ In a bowl, mix the edamame, ❶ and rice.
❸ Scoop ❷ into your hand and mold it into an onigiri of your preferred shape.

065 おせんべい

Senbei

［材料］

揚げせんべい…1/2枚、のり…1/8枚

❶ せんべいをビニール袋に入れ、手でたたいて細かく砕く。

❷ ご飯に❶をまぜ合わせて、俵形ににぎる。

❸ おにぎりをのりで巻く。

• 1/2 fried senbei

• 1/8 sheet nori

❶ Place the senbei in a plastic bag and crush with your hands.

❷ In a bowl, mix the senbei and rice and mold it into a tawara（cylinder-shaped）onigiri.

❸ Wrap ❷ with nori.

066 漬物ごま油炒め

［材料］
高菜漬け…大2、ごま油…小1
❶ 高菜漬けを細かく刻む。
❷ フライパンにごま油を入れ、中火で❶を炒める。
❸ ご飯に❷をまぜ合わせて、好きな形ににぎる。

• 1 tsp sesame oil, for the pan
• 2 tbsp takanazuke, finely chopped
❶ Heat the sesame oil in a pan over medium heat. Cook the takanazuke and mix with the rice.
❷ Scoop ❶ into your hand and mold it into an onigiri of your preferred shape.

3. 炊き込む・焼く

TAKIKOMI・GRILL

炊き込みご飯をつくる
HOW TO MAKE TAKIKOMI-GOHAN

炊き込みおにぎりをつくるために、まずは炊き込みご飯のつくり方を紹介します。お米に食材と調味料を入れて、ご飯を炊くだけという簡単な手順。食材の組み合わせは自由自在ですが、ポイントは食材から旨味がでるものを入れることです。

To make a takimi onigiri, you will first need to know how to make takikomi-gohan.Takikomi-gohan is mixed rice which is easily made by cooking rice with a variety of ingredients and seasonings. The trick is to add flavorful ingredients to extract that rich umami taste.

❶ 食材と調味料を用意します。

Prepare the ingredients and seasoning.

❷ お米と水の分量は1：1の同量です（レシピによっては水の量が変わる）。炊く前に30分くらい浸水させます。

Prepare equal amounts of rice and water. (Depending on the recipe, the amount of water may vary.) Steep the rice in water for approximately 30 minutes before cooking.

❸ 食材をお米の上に均等に広げ、調味料を加えます。

Place the ingredients evenly on top of the soaked rice and add the seasoning into the pot.

❹ ご飯の炊き方の手順通り（p.12参照）に炊きます。炊きあがったら、火をとめて10分蒸らします。

Cook the rice（see p.12）. Remove the pot from the heat, and let it steam for 10 minutes.

❺ 蒸らしたあと、ご飯と食材をよくまぜ合わせます。

When the rice is cooked, mix well.

067 ジャンバラヤ

Jambalaya

[材料]

米…1合、チキンブイヨン…160cc、チョリソー…1本、
赤ピーマン…1/3個、ピーマン…1/3個、トマト…小1個、
チリパウダー…小1、パプリカパウダー…小1、カレーパウダー…小1

❶ トマトはざく切り、ピーマン類は7㎜角に切り、チョリソーは7㎜の輪切りにする。

❷ 鍋に研いだ米とチキンブイヨンを入れ、30分吸水させる。

❸ チリパウダー、パプリカパウダー、カレーパウダーと❶を❷に入れて炊く。

❹ 炊きあがったら、よくまぜて好きな形ににぎる。

- 1 cup rice, washed　　• 160 ml chicken stock
- 1 chorizo, sliced into 7 mm coins
- 1/3 red bell pepper, sliced into 7 mm pieces
- 1/3 green bell pepper, sliced into 7 mm pieces
- 1 small tomato, coarsely chopped　　• 1 tsp chili powder
- 1tsp paprika powder　　• 1 tsp curry powder

❶ In a pot, steep the washed rice in the chicken stock for 30 minutes.

❷ Place the chorizo, peppers, tomato evenly in ❶ on top of the rice. Add the spices and cook the rice（see p.12）. When the rice is cooked, mix well.

❸ Scoop one serving of ❷ into your hand and mold it into an onigiri of your preferred shape.

068 しょうがご飯

Ginger Rice

[材料]

米…1合、だし汁…150cc、薄口醤油…大1/2、みりん…大1/2、
酒…大1/2、しょうが…30g

❶ しょうがは分量の半分をすりおろし、残りはみじん切りにする。

❷ 鍋に研いだ米とだし汁を入れ、30分吸水させる。

❸ 調味料とすりおろしの生姜を❷に入れて炊く。

❹ 炊き上がったら、みじん切りのしょうがを入れてまぜ、好きな形ににぎる。

• 1 cup rice, washed　　• 150 ml dashi　　• 1/2 tbsp light soy sauce
• 1/2 tbsp mirin　　• 1/2 tbsp sake　　• 15 grams ginger, freshly grated
• 15 grams ginger, minced

❶ In a pot, steep the washed rice in dashi for 30 minutes.

❷ Add the light soy sauce, mirin, sake, and grated ginger into ❶. Cook the rice (see p.12).

❸ Add the minced ginger into ❷ and mix well.

❹ Scoop one serving of ❸ into your hand and mold it into an onigiri of your preferred shape.

069 たこ飯

Octopus Rice

［材料］

米…1合、水…180cc、茹でたこ…足1本、醤油…大1/2、酒…大1/2、
しょうが…20g、昆布…5cm

❶ たこは一口大に切り、しょうがはせん切りにする。

❷ 鍋に研いだ米と水を入れ、30分吸水させる。

❸ 昆布、調味料、❶を❷に入れて炊く。

❹ 炊きあがったら昆布を取り出し、よくまぜて好きな形ににぎる。

• 1 cup rice, washed   • 180 ml water
• 1 octopus leg, cut into bite-size pieces   • 5 cm kombu
• 1/2 tbsp soy sauce   • 1/2 tbsp sake   • 20 grams ginger, julienned

❶ In a pot, steep the washed rice in the water for 30 minutes.

❷ Place the octopus and kombu evenly on top of the rice.

❸ Add the soy sauce, sake, and minced ginger in ❷ and cook the rice（see p.12）. When the rice is cooked, remove the kombu and mix well.

❹ Scoop one serving of ❸ into your hand and mold it into an onigiri of your preferred shape.

070 ツナ・トマトご飯

Canned Tuna & Tomato Rice

[材料]

米…1合、水…180cc、ツナ缶…50g、プチトマト…4個、
醤油…大1/2、酒…大1/2

❶ 鍋に研いだ米と水を入れ、30分吸水させる。

❷ ツナは水気を切り、形のままのプチトマトといっしょに❶に入れ、調味料
を入れて炊く。

❸ 炊きあがったらよくまぜて、好きな形ににぎる。

• 1 cup rice, washed　　• 180 ml water

• 50 grams canned tuna, squeeze out the excess liquid

• 4 cherry tomatoes　　• 1/2 tbsp soy sauce　　• 1/2 tbsp sake

❶ In a pot, steep the washed rice in the water for 30 minutes.

❷ Place the tuna and cherry tomatoes evenly in ❶ on top of the rice. Add the soy
sauce and sake and cook the rice（see p.12）. When the rice is cooked, mix well.

❸ Scoop one serving of ❷ into your hand and mold it into an onigiri of your
preferred shape.

071 ロゼご飯

Rosé Rice

［材料］

米…1合、水…90cc、ロゼワイン…90cc、塩…小1/2、

桜の花の塩漬け…3〜4本

❶ 桜の花の塩漬けはさっと洗い、水気を絞っておく。

❷ 鍋に研いだ米、水とロゼワインを入れ、30分吸水させる。

❸ 塩を❷に入れ、炊く。

❹ 炊きあがったら俵形ににぎり、上に桜の花をのせる。

• 1 cup rice, washed   • 90 ml water

• 90 ml rosé wine   • 1/2 tsp salt

• 3-4 salted cherry blossoms, washed with water and squeezed dry

❶ In a pot, steep the washed rice in water and rosé wine for 30 minutes.

❷ Add the salt and cook the rice (see p.12).

❸ Scoop one serving of ❷ into your hand and mold it into a tawara (cylinder-shaped) onigiri. Garnish with the salted cherry blossoms.

072 麦茶ご飯・アスパラ・枝豆

Barley Tea Rice, Asparagus & Edamame

［材料］

米1合、麦茶…180cc（p.203参照）、アスパラ…1本、枝豆…15粒

❶ アスパラと枝豆は固めに茹で、アスパラは5㎜の輪切りにする。

❷ 鍋に研いだ米と濃いめに煮出した麦茶を入れ、30分吸水させ、炊く。

❸ 麦茶ご飯が炊けたら、アスパラと枝豆を入れてよくまぜ、1〜2分蒸す。

❹ 蒸しあがったら、好きな形ににぎる。

- 1 cup rice, washed • 180 ml barley tea, brewed dark（see p.203）
- 1 asparagus spear, boiled firm, but not hard, and sliced into 5 mm pieces
- 15 edamame beans, boiled firmly in the pods, and shelled

❶ In a pot, steep the washed rice in dark barley tea for 30 minutes.

❷ Cook the rice（see p.12）.

❸ Mix the asparagus and edamame into ❷ and let it steam for 1-2 minutes.

❹ Scoop one serving of ❸ into your hand and mold it into an onigiri of your preferred shape.

073 大根めし

Daikon Rice

［材料］

米…1合、水…180cc、大根…80g、大根の葉…15g、油揚げ…15g、塩…小1/2、薄口醤油…小1、酒…小1

❶ 大根は2㎝の短冊切り、油揚げはせん切りにする。

❷ 大根の葉はみじん切りにして、分量外の塩少々で軽くもみ、水気を絞っておく。

❸ 鍋に研いだお米と水を入れて、30分吸水させる。

❹ 調味料と大根、油揚げを❸に入れて、炊く。

❺ 炊きあがったら、❷を入れてよくまぜ、好きな形ににぎる。

• 1 cup rice, washed　　• 180 ml water
• 80 grams daikon, skinned, and cut into 2 cm rectangles
• 15 grams deep-fried tofu, julienned　　• 1 tsp light soy sauce　　• 1 tsp sake
• 1/2 tsp salt　　• 15 grams daikon greens, minced and rubbed with salt

❶ In a pot, steep the washed rice in the water for 30 minutes.

❷ Place the daikon and deep-fried tofu evenly in ❶ on top of the rice. Add the soy sauce, sake, and salt and cook the rice (see p.12).

❸ Drain the excess liquid from the minced daikon greens and mix well in ❷.

❹ Scoop one serving of ❸ into your hand and mold it into an onigiri of your preferred shape.

074 鶏きのこご飯

Chicken & Kinoko Mushroom Rice

[材料]

米…1合、水…180cc、鶏肉（ももか胸どちらでも）…40g、
しめじ…1/4パック、エリンギ…1/4パック、えのき…1/4パック、人参…20g、
酒…20cc、醤油…小1、塩…少々

❶ しめじはほぐし、エリンギは2cmほどの長さで薄くスライスする。えのきは
半分の長さに切り、人参はせん切りにする。

❷ 鶏肉は小さく切り、分量とは別の酒と塩少々を振りかけておく。

❸ 鍋に研いだ米と水を入れて、30分吸水させる。

❹ 調味料と❶と❷を❸に入れて、炊く。

❺ 炊きあがったら、よくまぜて好きな形ににぎる。

- 1 cup rice, washed　　• 180 ml water
- 40 grams chicken breast or thigh, cut into small pieces, drizzle some sake and lightly salt
- 20 grams shimeji mushroom, broken apart
- 20 grams eringi mushroom, thinly sliced　　• 20 grams enoki mushroom, cut in half
- 20 grams carrot, julienned　　• 20 ml sake, for the rice
- 1 tsp soy sauce　　• 1/2 tsp salt, for the rice

❶ In a pot, steep the washed rice in water for 30 minutes.

❷ Place the chicken and the mushrooms evenly in ❶ on top of the rice. Add the soy sauce, sake and salt and cook the rice (see p.12). When the rice is cooked, mix well.

❸ Scoop one serving of ❷ into your hand and mold it into an onigiri of your preferred shape.

075 お赤飯

Osekihan

［材料］

もち米…1.5合、米…0.5合、水…360cc、
小豆…1/4合、黒ごま…大1

❶ 小豆を鍋に入れて、水に最低でも3時間は浸す。

❷ 小豆をかぶるくらいの水で茹で、いったん茹でこぼし、灰汁をとる。

❸ 再び小豆の3倍の水を入れて20分くらい煮る。

❹ 煮上がったら、茹で汁と小豆に分け、茹で汁は捨てずにとっておく。

❺ 鍋に研いだ米ともち米、小豆を入れる。とっておいた茹で汁に水をたし360ccにし、入れて炊く。

❻ 炊きあがったら、まぜて好きな形ににぎる。黒ごまをその上にまぶす。

• 1/4 cup azuki beans, soaked in a pot of water for at least 3 hours.
• 1 1/2 cups sweet (sticky) rice, washed
• 1/2 cup rice
• 1 tbsp black sesame

❶ In a pot, cover the azuki beans with water and bring to a boil. Skim the surface and drain the water.

❷ Add 1 cup of water and let it simmer over low heat for 20 minutes. Take out the azuki beans but save the broth.

❸ Take the broth and add some water to make 360 ml of liquid.

❹ In a pot, add the washed sticky rice, azuki beans to ❸ and cook the rice (see p.12).

❺ Scoop one serving of ❹ into your hand and mold it into an onigiri of your preferred shape. Sprinkle some black sesame on the surface.

★Osekihan is a traditional celebratory dish made from azuki beans and sticky rice.

焼きおにぎりをつくる
HOW TO MAKE GRILLED ONIGIRI

おにぎりをにぎった後に、タレをつけて焼く「焼きおにぎり」。焼くことでご飯が香ばしくなり、ぱりっとした食感も楽しめます。焼きたてのあつあつの美味しさは格別です。タレのバリエーションを考えてオリジナルにも挑戦してみてください。

Yaki onigiri, or grilled onigiri, is onigiri glazed with savory sauce and grilled on a pan or a barbecue grill. Fresh off the grill, the onigiri, with a sweet burnt aroma and a crispy crust, is simply irresistible. Be creative and try experimenting with a variation on the sauce.

❶ タレの材料（p.135参照）をよくまぜ合わせ、おにぎりに刷毛でタレを塗ります。

Make the sauce and glaze the surface of the onigiri with a brush（see p.135）.

❷ オーブントースターやグリルで、おにぎりを2〜3分焼きます（火力の強さで焼き上がる時間が異なります）。

Lightly grease the grill or oven toaster, and heat at medium heat. Place the onigiri on the grill, and roast for 2-3 minutes. Cooking time may vary depending on the heat level.

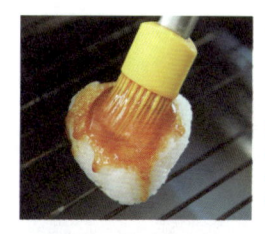

❸ もう一度タレを塗り、1分程度、焼き目がこんがりするくらいに焼きます。

Remove the onigiri and glaze the surface again with the sauce. Put it back on to the grill for another minute until lightly browned on both sides.

❹ 焼き具合はお好みですが、タレにお砂糖などが入っている場合は焦げやすいので注意。

Grill according to your preference for crispiness. If the sauce contains sugar, note the surface may burn faster.

Tips: 網にホイルをしいて焼くとくっつきにくくなります。フライパンで焼くときは薄くサラダ油をひいて、両面を中火でこんがりと焼きます。

If the onigiri continues to stick to the grill, use aluminum foil. When using a pan, lightly grease and heat over medium heat. Cook both sides of the onigiri until browned.

076 焼きおにぎりバーガー

Grilled Onigiri Burger

[材料]
ハンバーグ…1個、レタス…1/4枚、サラダ油…少々

❶ ハンバーグのつくり方はp.181を参照。

❷ おにぎり1個分のご飯を2等分にし、丸く平らににぎる。

❸ サラダ油を薄くひいたフライパンで❷を焦げ目がつくように焼く。

❹ レタスとハンバーグを❸ではさむ。

• 1 salisbury steak　　• 1/4 piece lettuce
• 1/2 tsp cooking oil, for the pan or grill

❶ See p.181 for salisbury steak recipe.
❷ Scoop one serving of rice, divide in half and flatten them into a patty shape.
❸ Lightly grease and heat the grill or pan over medium heat and cook ❷ until browned.
❹ Place the lettuce and burger between the patty-shaped onigiri.

077 味噌焼きおにぎり

Grilled Miso Onigiri

[材料]

味噌…大1、砂糖…大1、みりん…大1、ごま…少々、サラダ油…少々

❶ 材料の調味料をすべてよくまぜ合わせる。

❷ 基本のおにぎりをにぎる。

❸ ❷に❶を塗り、オーブントースターまたはサラダ油を薄くひいたフライパンでこんがりと焼き、ごまをかける。

• 1 tbsp miso　　• 1 tbsp sugar　　• 1 tbsp mirin　　• 1/2 tsp sesame
• 1/2 tsp cooking oil for the pan or grill

❶ Scoop one serving of rice and mold it into a triangular onigiri.

❷ In a bowl, mix the miso, sugar, mirin, and sesame.

❸ Glaze the surface of ❶ with ❷ and cook it on a lightly greased grill or pan until lightly browned on both sides.

078 焼きおにぎり・サルサソース
Grilled Onigiri with Salsa Sauce

[材料]
サルサソース（市販のもの）…小2、コリアンダー…少々
サラダ油…少々
❶ 平らな丸形おにぎりをにぎる。
❷ オーブントースターまたはサラダ油を薄くひいたフライパ
ンで、❶の両面を焼く。
❸ ❷の上にサルサソースをのせて、コリアンダーを飾る。

・2 tsp salsa sauce
・1 fresh coriander leaf
・1/2 tsp cooking oil for the pan or grill
❶ Scoop one serving of rice and mold it into a coin-shaped onigiri.
❷ Lightly grease and heat the grill or frying pan over medium heat and cook the onigiri for 2-3 minutes.
❸ Drizzle the salsa sauce on ❷ and top it with the coriander leaf.

079 ピーナッツバター焼きおにぎり
Peanut Butter Grilled Onigiri

［材料］
ピーナッツバター…大1、はちみつ…大1
❶ ピーナッツバターとはちみつをよくまぜる。
❷ 平らな丸形おにぎりをにぎる。
❸ オーブントースターで軽くおにぎりを焼き、❶を塗りもう一度
こんがりと焼く。

- 1 tbsp peanut butter
- 1 tbsp honey
- 1/2 tsp cooking oil for the pan or grill
❶ In a bowl, mix the peanut butter and honey.
❷ Scoop one serving of rice and mold it into a coin-shaped onigiri.
❸ Cook ❷ on a lightly greased grill or pan, then glaze the surface with ❶.
❹ Grill ❸ again until lightly browned on both sides.

4. のせる・つつむ
SUSHI-STYLE・WRAP

にぎってのせる

HOW TO MAKE SUSHI-STYLE ONIGIRI

にぎったおにぎりの上に具材をのせるにぎり寿司スタイルのおにぎり。にぎり方は丸形や俵形など、上にのせる具材の形や軟らかさなどで決めるのがいいでしょう。具材のバリエーションを楽しみましょう。

The round or tawara onigiri is the ideal shape for making sushi-style onigiri. Choose either shape depending on the topping. Enjoy the variety of toppings you can use to make sushi-style onigiri.

❶ ご飯を俵形ににぎります。

Make a tawara onigiri.

❷ 上に具材をのせたら、軽く具材を押さえるようにもう一度にぎります。

Place the topping on the onigiri and gently press down.

❸ できあがったおにぎりに、トッピングを飾ったり、のりや野菜を巻いたりお好みでどうぞ。

Top the onigiri with garnish, or wrap it with nori or vegetables as you like.

080 ローストビーフ

Roast Beef

［材料］

ローストビーフ…1切れ、大葉…1枚、練り辛子…少々

❶ ローストビーフのつくり方はp.182を参照。

❷ ご飯を俵形ににぎる。

❸ 半分に切った大葉、ローストビーフを❷にのせ、練り辛子をそえる。

• 1 slice roast beef　　• 1 ooba, cut in half

• 1/4 tsp karashi paste

❶ See p.182 for roast beef recipe.

❷ Scoop one serving of rice and mold it into a tawara (cylinder-shaped) onigiri.

❸ Place the ooba and roast beef on ❷ and garnish with karashi paste.

甘酢れんこん

Sweet Vinegar Lotus Root

［材料］
甘酢れんこん…1枚、アスパラ（茹でたもの）…輪切り1枚、すし酢…小2
❶ 甘酢れんこんのつくり方はp.183を参照。
❷ ご飯にすし酢をまぜ、俵形ににぎる。
❸ 甘酢れんこん1枚を❷の上にのせ、その上に小さくスライスしたアスパラをのせる。

• 1 slice sweet vinegar lotus root　　• 2 tsp sushi vinegar
• 1 asparagus spear, boiled and sliced into small pieces
❶ See p.183 for sweet vinegar lotus root recipe.
❷ In a bowl, mix the vinegar and rice and mold it into a tawara (cylinder-shaped) onigiri.
❸ Place the sweet vinegar lotus root and asparagus on top of ❷.

082 カレーピラフ風海老のせ

Curry & Shrimp

[材料]
カレーパウダー…小1/2、バター…小1、中濃ソース…小1/2、海老…1尾

❶ 海老は茹でる。

❷ フライパンにバターを入れ、中火でご飯を炒め、カレーパウダー、中濃ソースで味付けをする。

❸ ❷を俵形ににぎり、その上に海老をのせ、もう一度押さえるようににぎる。

• 1 tsp butter, for the pan　　• 1/2 tsp curry powder
• 1/2 tsp semi-thick Worcestershire sauce　　• 1 shrimp, boiled

❶ Heat the butter in a pan over medium heat and stir-fry the rice. Season with curry powder and semi-thick Worcestershire sauce.

❷ Scoop the rice and mold it into a tawara (cylinder-shaped) onigiri.

❸ Place the boiled shrimp on top of ❷ and gently press down.

083 しいたけ

Shiitake

［材料］

しいたけ…1枚、醤油…小1/2、炒り卵…大1、サラダ油…少々、塩…少々

❶ しいたけをグリルまたはフライパンでさっと焼き、醤油で味をつける。

❷ フライパンに薄くサラダ油をひいて、塩を加えた卵をよくかきまぜ、炒り卵をつくる。

❸ ご飯と❷をまぜ合わせ、丸形ににぎる。

❹ ❶を❸にのせる。

• 1 shiitake cap   • 1/2 tsp soy sauce   • 1/2 tsp cooking oil, for the pan
• a pinch of salt   • 1 egg, cracked and beaten

❶ Lightly grill the shiitake on a grill or a pan and season with the soy sauce.

❷ Heat the oil in a pan over medium heat. Add a pinch of salt into the egg and pour the mixture into the pan. Move the mixture with a spatula to make a scrambled egg.

❸ In a bowl, mix ❷ and rice and mold it into a round onigiri.

❹ Place ❶ on top of ❸.

084 スモークサーモン手まり寿司

Smoked Salmon Ball

［材料］
スモークサーモン…1枚、ケッパー…1 〜 2粒、すし酢…小1
❶ ご飯にすし酢をまぜ合わせ、ピンポン玉大に丸くにぎる。
❷ ラップを広げ、その上にスモークサーモンとケッパーをのせ、最後に❶
をおき、ラップをしぼって丸形にする。

• 1 tsp sushi vinegar • 1 slice smoked salmon
• 1-2 capers • 1 radish sprout
❶ In a bowl, mix the sushi vinegar and rice and mold it into a ping pong-like ball.
❷ Cut a sheet of saran wrap and place the smoked salmon and caper on it.
Place ❶ on top of everything and close the saran wrap and mold it into a ball.
❸ Take off the saran wrap and top with the radish sprout.

085 キムチ・スパム

Kimchi & Spam

[材料]
キムチ…大2、スパム…1切れ
❶ ご飯にキムチを刻んでまぜ、俵形ににぎる。
❷ スパムはフライパンでこんがり焼く。
❸ ❶に❷をのせて、上からピックで押さえる。

• 2 tbsp kimchi, finely chopped
• 1 slice spam
❶ In a bowl, mix the kimchi and rice and mold it into
a tawara (cylinder-shaped) onigiri.
❷ Heat a pan over medium heat and grill the spam.
❸ Place ❷ on ❶ and pierce it with a pick to hold
together.

086 パプリカのせ

Paprika

［材料］

パプリカ…1/6個、塩…少々、オリーブオイル…小1/2

❶ パプリカをオーブントースターで焼き、皮をむいて、2㎝幅に切る。

❷ ❶に塩を少しふり、オリーブオイルをまぶす。

❸ ご飯を俵形ににぎり、その上に❷をのせる。

• 1 /6 paprika　　• a pinch of salt　　• 1/2 tsp olive oil

❶ Heat the paprika in the oven toaster for about 10 minutes. Peel the skin and cut into 2 cm pieces.

❷ Sprinkle some salt on ❶ and drizzle some olive oil.

❸ Scoop the rice into your hand and mold it into a tawara（cylinder-shaped）onigiri.

❹ Place ❷ on ❸.

087 エリンギ

Eringi

［材料］
エリンギ…スライス1枚、バター…少々、黒こしょう…適宜、のり…1/8枚
❶ 薄くスライスしたエリンギをバターで炒め、黒こしょうをふる。
❷ ご飯を俵形ににぎる。
❸ ❷に❶をのせて、のりを帯にまく。

• 1 slice eringi, sliced into thin piece　　• 1/4 tsp butter
• a pinch of black pepper　　• 1/8 sheet nori
❶ Heat a pan over medium heat and cook the sliced eringi with butter and black pepper.
❷ Scoop the rice into your hand and mold it into a tawara（cylinder-shaped）onigiri.
❸ Place ❶ on ❷ and wrap the nori around it.

にぎってつつむ

HOW TO MAKE WRAPPED ONIGIRI

つつみおにぎりの場合は、おにぎりを丸形や俵形などにするとつつみやすくなります。つつむ素材によって巻き方を変えるなど、組み合わせを考えるのも楽しいでしょう。

Round or tawara onigiri is the ideal shape for making wrapped onigiri. Experiment with different ways of wrapping your onigiri depending on your choice of wrapper.

葉物でおにぎりを包む方法 Wrap with Greens

❶ さっと茹でたレタスの水気をよく切り、手のひらにのせ、真ん中におにぎりをのせる。

Lightly boil the lettuce, drain, and dry well. Hold the lettuce in your hand and place the onigiri on the lettuce.

❷ おにぎりが隠れるように丸く包みます。

Wrap the lettuce around the onigiri to cover the rice.

❸ 手まり形のレタス包みの完成です。他にも、茹でたチンゲン菜、野沢菜や高菜の漬物など、大きな葉ものが向いています。

Other leafy ingredients such as boiled bok choy, pickled nozawana, takanazuke, and greens with large leaves can be used as wraps in lieu of lettuce.

野菜をおにぎりに巻く方法 Wrap Around with Vegetable Strips

❶ ミントを入れたご飯を俵形ににぎります。

Make a tawara（cylinder-shaped）onigiri using rice with mint.

❷ 薄くスライスしたズッキーニに軽く塩をして、しんなりしたら、おにぎりの側面に巻きつけます。これは軍艦巻きといいます。

Slice zucchini into thin strips and sprinkle some salt. Wrap the side of the onigiri with the zucchini. This is called gunkan-style.

❸ ほかにも、きゅうりや人参、大根のスライスなどを使って、軍艦巻きだけでなく、帯として巻くことも出来ます。

Some alternative wraps are thin strips of cucumbers, carrots, and daikon. You can also strap it over the rice like a belt.

088 うなきゅう

Cucumber Unagi

[材料]

うなぎ…20g、きゅうり…スライス1枚、
スパイスオイル…小1（p.203参照）、塩…少々

❶ きゅうりをピーラーで薄くスライスし、塩をふる。
❷ うなぎは1cm幅に切る。
❸ ご飯にスパイスオイルをまぜ合わせ、うなぎもまぜる。
❹ ❸を俵形ににぎり、きゅうりを帯にして巻く。

• 1 tsp spice oil（see p.203） • 20 grams unagi, cut into 1 cm pieces
• 1 thin slice cucumber（use a peeler）, salted • 1/4 tsp salt

❶ In a bowl, mix the spice oil, unagi, and rice and mold it into a tawara （cylinder-shaped） onigiri.
❷ Strap ❶ with cucumber, belt-style.

089 桜の葉つつみ

Salted Cherry Blossom Leaf Wrap

［材料］
梅酢…小2、桜の葉（塩漬け）…1枚
❶ ご飯に梅酢をあえ、俵形ににぎる。
❷ 桜の葉で❶をつつむ。

• 2 tsp umezu vinegar
• 1 salted cherry blossom leaf
❶ In a bowl, mix the umezu vinegar and rice and mold it into a tawara（cylinder-shaped）onigiri.
❷ Wrap ❶ with the salted cherry blossom leaf.

090 黒こしょう・オリーブのりはさみ

Black Pepper & Olive Nori

[材料]
黒こしょう…小1、オリーブのり…1枚（p.203参照）
❶ ご飯に黒こしょうをまぜ、俵形ににぎる。
❷ オリーブのりで❶をはさむ。

• 1 tsp black pepper
• 1 sheet olive nori (see p.203)
❶ In a bowl, mix the black pepper and rice and mold it into a tawara (cylinder-shaped) onigiri.
❷ Wrap ❶ with olive nori.

091 ミックスビーンズ ・ 生春巻き
Mixed Beans Spring Roll

［材料］
ミックスビーンズ（茹でてあるもの）…大1、レタス…1/2枚、
ポン酢ジュレ…小2、生春巻きの皮…小1枚
❶ ミックスビーンズを半量のポン酢ジュレであえる。
❷ ご飯に❶をまぜ合わせる。
❸ 湿らせた生春巻きの皮の上にレタスをしき、その上に❷をのせ、巻く。
残りのポン酢ジュレをつけて食べる。

• 1 tbsp canned mixed beans　　• 2 tsp ponzu gelée　　• 1/2 piece lettuce
• 1 sheet rice paper, damped with water until soft
❶ In a bowl, mix half of the ponzu gelée into the mixed beans.
❷ Mix ❶ with rice.
❸ Place the lettuce on the rice paper and place ❷ on top of the lettuce and wrap
up. Use the rest of the ponzu gelée as the dip.

092 柚子ご飯・白菜つつみ
Yuzu Rice Wrapped in Chinese Cabbage

[材料]
柚子の皮…小1、白菜の漬物…1枚
❶ 柚子の皮はせん切りにする。
❷ ご飯に柚子の皮のせん切りをまぜ合わせる。
❸ ❶を丸形ににぎり、白菜の漬物でつつむ。

• 1 tsp yuzu rind, julienned
• 1 piece Chinese cabbage, pickled
❶ In a bowl, mix the yuzu rind and rice and mold it into a round onigiri.
❷ Wrap ❶ with Chinese cabbage.

093 ミントご飯・ズッキーニ巻き

Mint Rice Wrapped in Zucchini

［材料］

ミント…10g、ズッキーニ…スライス1枚、塩…少々

❶ ご飯にミントをまぜ合わせて、俵形ににぎる。

❷ ズッキーニをピーラーで薄くスライスし、塩を少々ふってしんなりさせる。

❸ ❶を❷で巻く。

• 10 grams mint leaves　• 1 thin slice zucchini（use a peeler）, salted
• a pinch of salt
❶ In a bowl, mix the mint and rice and mold it into a tawara（cylinder-shaped）
onigiri.
❷ Wrap ❶ with zucchini.

094 めはり

Mehari

［材料］
高菜の漬け物…1枚
❶ ご飯を丸形ににぎる。
❷ 高菜漬けで❶をつつむ。

• 1 slice takanazuke
❶ Scoop one serving of rice and mold it into a round onigiri.
❷ Wrap ❶ with the takanazuke.

095 モッツァレーラチーズ・生ハムつつみ

Mozzarella Cheese Wrapped in Prosciutto

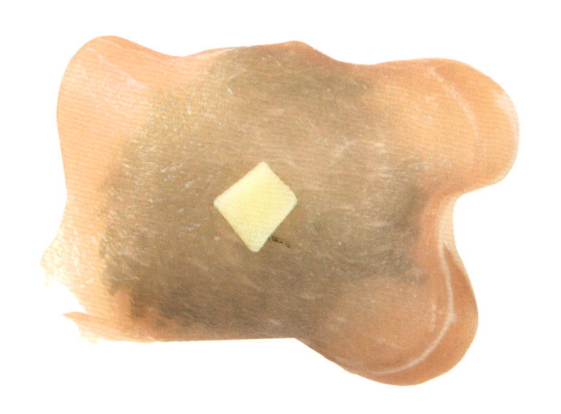

［材料］
生ハム…1枚、モッツァレーラチーズ…10g、大葉…1枚、ごま…少々
❶ モッツァレーラチーズを1㎝角に切り、ひとかけを残し、ごまと一緒にご飯にまぜ合わせる。
❷ ❶を丸形ににぎる。
❸ ❷を大葉、生ハムの順でつつむ。上にモッツァレーラチーズひとかけをのせる。

• 10 grams mozzarella cheese, chopped into 1 cm cubes
• 1 ooba　　• 1/4 tsp white sesame　　• 1 slice prosciutto
❶ Set a cube of mozzarella cheese aside. In a bowl, mix the rest of the mozzarella cubes, sesame, and rice and mold it into a round onigiri.
❷ Wrap ❶ with ooba, then wrap everything with prosciutto.
❸ Place the mozzarella cube from ❶ on top of ❷.

096 オイルサーディン・レタスつつみ

Oiled Sardine Wrapped in Lettuce

[材料]
オイルサーディン（缶詰）…1切れ、レタス…1枚
❶ レタスを軽く茹でて水気を切る。
❷ ご飯は俵形ににぎる。
❸ ❷にオイルサーディンをのせ、❶でつつむ。

• 1 fillet canned sardines in oil
• 1 piece lettuce, boiled and wiped dry
❶ Scoop one serving of rice and mold it into a tawara (cylinder-shaped) onigiri.
❷ Place the sardines on ❶ and wrap with the lettuce.

097 コチジャン・えごま

Gochujang & Egoma

[材料]
コチジャン…小2、みりん…小1/2、えごまの葉…1枚

❶ コチジャンにみりんを入れてのばす。

❷ 基本のおにぎりをにぎり、片面に❶を塗り、オーブントースターまたはフライパンで両面をこんがり焼く。

❸ えごまの葉で❷をつつむ。

• 2 tsp gochujang　　• 1/2 tsp mirin　　• 1 egoma perilla leaf

❶ In a bowl, mix the gochujang and mirin.

❷ Scoop one serving of rice and mold it into a triangular onigiri.

❸ Glaze one side of ❷ with ❶ and grill it on a heated grill or pan until lightly browned.

❹ Wrap ❸ with egoma perilla leaf.

肉味噌・レタスつつみ

Nikumiso Wrapped in Lettuce

［材料］
肉味噌…大2、レタス…1枚
❶ 肉味噌のつくり方はp.184を参照。
❷ レタスを軽く茹でて、水気をとる。
❸ ご飯に❶をまぜ合わせて、丸形おにぎりをにぎる。
❹ ❸を❷でつつむ。

• 2 tbsp nikumiso　　• 1 piece lettuce, boiled and wiped dry
❶ See p.184 for nikumiso recipe.
❷ In a bowl, mix ❶ and rice and mold it into a round onigiri.
❸ Wrap ❷ with lettuce.

099 ベーコン・薄焼き卵巻き

Bacon Wrapped in Egg

［材料］

ベーコン…1/2枚、薄焼き卵…1枚

❶ 薄焼き卵のつくり方はp.185を参照。

❷ ベーコンは細かく刻んで、フライパンでカリカリに焼く。飾り用に少し残しておく。

❸ ご飯に❷をまぜ合わせ、俵形ににぎる。

❹ 薄焼き卵の中央に❸をのせてつつむ。

❺ 薄焼き卵の真ん中にバッテンの切り込みを入れ、ベーコンで飾る。

• 1 usuyaki tamago（thin omlette）　　• 1/2 slice bacon, finely chopped

❶ See p.185 for usuyaki tamago recipe.

❷ Heat a pan over medium heat and cook the bacon until browned and crispy. Set aside some bacon for garnish.

❸ In a bowl, mix the rest of the bacon and rice and mold it into a tawara（cylinder-shaped）onigiri.

❹ Wrap the thin omlette around ❸.

❺ Using a knife, cut an "x" into the center of ❹ and garnish with the bacon that was set aside.

100 のりの佃煮マヨ・大葉はさみ

Nori Tsukudani & Mayo Wrapped with Ooba

[材料]
のりの佃煮…小1、マヨネーズ…小1、大葉…2枚

❶ のりの佃煮とマヨネーズをまぜ合わせる。

❷ 基本のおにぎりをにぎり、真ん中に❶を入れる。

❸ 2枚の大葉ではさむ。

• 1 tsp nori tsukudani
• 1 tsp mayonnaise
• 2 ooba leaves

❶ In a bowl, mix the nori tsukudani and mayonnaise.

❷ Scoop one serving of rice, put ❶ in the center and mold it into an onigiri of your preferred shape.

❸ Sandwich ❷ with ooba leaves.

101 フライドオニオン・肉巻き

［材料］
薄切り牛肉…2枚、フライドオニオン（市販のもの）…大1、醤油…小2、
酒…小1、みりん…小1、サラダ油…小1/2

❶ ご飯にフライドオニオンをまぜて、俵形ににぎる。フライドオニオンは飾り用に少し残しておく。

❷ 薄切り牛肉を❶に巻く。

❸ フライパンに薄くサラダ油をひいて、❷を焼き色がつくまで焼き、調味料で味をつける。

❹ 出来上がったら、フライドオニオンを上にのせる。

• 1 tbsp fried onion flakes • 2 thinly sliced sirloin beef
• 1/2 tsp cooking oil, for the pan • 2 tsp soy sauce
• 1 tsp sake • 1 tsp mirin

❶ Set aside some fried onion flakes for garnish. In a bowl, mix the rest of it with rice and mold it into a tawara (cylinder-shaped) onigiri.

❷ Wrap the beef slices around ❶.

❸ Heat the oil in a pan over medium heat, and cook ❷ until lightly browned. Season with the sake, soy sauce, and mirin.

❹ Garnish with the fried onion flakes set aside from ❶.

おかずレシピ
OKAZU RECIPE

おにぎりに使った具材の中で、調理が必要なおかずのレシピを紹介します。分量はご飯のおかずとして、単品で食べる場合の2人分を目安にしています。

Okazu means side dishes accompanying rice and other carbohydrates. Here, we introduce okazu recipes to use as onigiri fillings. All the recipes make two servings.

1. 麻婆豆腐 [p.44]
Mapo Tofu

[材料]
豆腐…400g、豚ひき肉…100g、長ネギ…1本、しょうが…小1、ニンニク…小1、豆板醤…小1、酒…大2、砂糖…小2、醤油…小2、チキンコンソメ…少々、水…150cc、片栗粉・水…各大1、サラダ油…小1

❶ 豆腐は一口大に切る。長ネギ、しょうが、ニンニクはみじん切り。

❷ 中華鍋にサラダ油をひいて、弱火で長ネギ、しょうが、ニンニク、豆板醤を順に入れ、強火にして香りをだす。

❸ 豚ひき肉を入れてよく炒め、残りの調味料と水を加える。

❹ 沸騰したら豆腐を加えて、再び沸騰するのを待ち、水で溶いた片栗粉を入れよくかきまぜる。

- 1 tsp cooking oil, for the wok
- 1 leek, minced
- 1 tsp ginger, minced
- 1 tsp garlic, minced
- 1 tsp doubanjiang
- 100 grams ground pork
- 2 tbsp sake
- 2 tsp sugar
- 2 tsp soy sauce
- 1/2 tsp chicken stock
- 150 ml water
- 400 grams silken tofu, cut into bite-sized pieces
- 1 tbsp potato starch, mixed in 1 tbsp water

❶ Heat the cooking oil in a wok over low heat and add the leek, ginger, garlic, and doubanjiang. Raise the heat to high.

1

2

❷ Add the ground pork to ❶ and sauté. Then add sake, sugar, soy sauce, stock, and water.
❸ Once the mixture boils, add the tofu. When it starts to boil again, add the starch and mix well.

2. すき焼き [p.46]
Sukiyaki

[材料]
牛肉…150g、長ネギ…1本、しらたき…50g、焼き豆腐または木綿豆腐…200g、割り下（醤油…30cc、みりん…30cc、砂糖…大1、水…150cc）、サラダ油…少々
❶ 割り下の材料を鍋に入れ、中火で沸騰するまで煮立てる。
❷ 牛肉、豆腐 は一口大に切る。長ネギは斜め切り。しらたきは下

茹でする。
❸ 鍋にサラダ油をひいて、強火で肉を焼き、続いて長ネギと豆腐としらたきを入れて、❶を注ぎ、沸騰したら中火にして4、5分煮る。

- -

sukiyaki stock:
• 30 ml soy sauce
• 30 ml mirin
• 1 tbsp sugar
• 150 ml water

- -

• 1/2 tsp cooking oil, for the large pot
• 150 grams sukiyaki beef, cut into bite-size pieces
• 1 leek, diagonally sliced
• 200 grams grilled tofu or firm tofu
• 50 grams shirataki, lightly boiled

❶ Heat the sukiyaki stock in a pot over medium heat until it boils.
❷ Heat the cooking oil in a large pot over high heat and cook the beef until browned. Add leek, tofu, shirataki and pour in ❶. Turn down to medium heat when the mixture comes to a boil. Let it cook for 4-5 minutes.

3. から揚げ [p.48]

Karaage（Deep-Fried Chicken）

［材料］
鶏のもも肉…250g、ニンニク（すりおろし）…小1、醤油…大1、酒…大1、片栗粉…大3、小麦粉…大3、サラダ油（揚げ用）…適宜
❶ 鶏肉は一口大に切り、ニンニク、醤油、酒をよくもみ込む。

❷ 片栗粉と小麦粉をまぜ合わせて、鶏肉にまぶして170度の油でこんがりと揚げる。

• 250 grams chicken thighs, cut into bite-size pieces
• 1 tsp grated garlic
• 1 tbsp soy sauce
• 1 tbsp sake
• 3 tbsp potato starch
• 3 tbsp flour
• 2 cups cooking oil, for deep frying

❶ Massage the chicken with garlic, soy sauce, and sake.
❷ In a bowl, mix the potato starch and flour, and coat the chicken.
❸ Deep fry the chicken in 170°C oil.

3

4

4. 黒豆煮 [p.49]

Sweet Simmered Black Beans

［材料］
黒豆…2カップ、砂糖…2と1/2カップ、醤油…大1、水…8カップ、錆びた釘…2〜3本

❶ 黒豆は豆の4倍量の水（8カップ）に一晩浸す。洗ってガーゼで包んだ錆びた釘も一緒に入れる。

❷ そのまま強火にかける。沸騰したら灰汁を取り、水を差す。豆が水から出ないように、何度かくり返す。

❸ 灰汁が出なくなったら、弱火にして約1時間煮る。

❹ 豆が指で潰せるくらい軟らかくなったら、釘を取り出して砂糖を入れ、弱火で20分くらい煮る。

❺ 最後に醤油を入れて、そのまま蓋をして冷ます。

- - - - - - - - - - - - - - - - - - - -

• 2 cups black beans
• 8 cups water
• 2-3 rusty iron nails, cleaned and wrapped with paper towel
• 2 1/2 cups sugar
• 1 tbsp soy sauce

- - - - - - - - - - - - - - - - - - - -

❶ In a pot, soak the black beans in 8 cups of water overnight. Add the wrapped nails.

❷ Boil ❶ over high heat. Skim the surface and add some water. The beans should be covered with water at all times.

❸ Continue to skim and add water several times until no more scum rises to the surface. Turn down to low heat and cook for an hour.

❹ When the beans are soft enough to crush between your fingers, remove the nails

5

and add the sugar. Continue to cook over low heat for 20 minutes.
❺ Add the soy sauce and turn off the heat. Let the pot sit and cool.

5. こんにゃく甘辛煮 [p.51]
Sweet-and-Salty Konnyaku

［材料］

こんにゃく…1/2枚、酒…小2、みりん…小2、砂糖…小2、ごま油…小1、赤唐辛子（刻む）…少々

❶ こんにゃくは熱湯をかけて、短冊に切る。
❷ 鍋にごま油をひき、中火で赤唐辛子、こんにゃくを炒めてから、すべての調味料を入れて汁気がなくなるまで炒める。

- - - - - - - - - - - - - - - - - - -

• 1/2 slice konnyaku
• 1 tsp sesame oil, for the pan

• 2 tsp sake
• 2 tsp mirin
• 2 tsp sugar
• 1/2 tsp red chile pepper, chopped

- - - - - - - - - - - - - - - - - - -

❶ Pour hot water over the konnyaku and cut into rectangular slices.
❷ In a pan, heat the sesame oil over medium heat and stir-fry ❶. Then mix in the sake, mirin, sugar, and chile pepper and stir-fry until the liquid evaporates.

6. きんぴら [p.54]
Kinpira（Burdock and Carrot Sauté）

［材料］

ごぼう…1本（150gくらい）、人参…1/3 本（60gくらい）、醤油…大1と1/2、みりん…大1、砂糖…

6

7

小2、ごま油…小2
❶ ごぼうと人参はマッチ棒状の粗めのせん切りにし、鍋にごま油をひき、中火で炒める。
❷ 調味料を加え、水気がなくなるまで炒める。

- -

• 2 tsp sesame oil, for the pot
• 150 grams burdock, cut into matchsticks
• 60 grams carrot, cut into matchsticks
• 1 1/2 tbsp soy sauce
• 1 tbsp mirin
• 2 tsp sugar

- -

❶ Heat the sesame oil in a pot over medium heat and sauté the burdock and carrot.
❷ Add the soy sauce, mirin, and sugar and sauté until the liquid evaporates.

7. しゅうまい [p.58]

Shumai Dumpling

[材料]
豚ひき肉…150g、玉ねぎ…25g、帆立の水煮缶 …15g、中華スープの素…小1/2、ごま油…小1、小麦粉…小1、しゅうまいの皮…10枚

❶ 玉ねぎはみじん切りにし、しゅうまいの皮以外の材料をすべてまぜ、よくこねる。
❷ しゅうまいの皮に❶をのせて包み、湯気の上がった蒸し器で5分蒸す。

- -

• 1 tsp flour
• 25 grams onion, minced
• 150 grams ground pork
• 15 grams canned plain boiled scallops
• 1/2 tsp soup stock granules
• 1 tsp sesame oil

8

• 10 dumpling skins

❶ Mix the flour into the onions. Add the pork, scallops, soup stock and sesame oil and mix well.

❷ Wrap ❶ with dumpling skins and steam using a steamer for 5 minutes.

8. 新しょうがの甘酢漬け [p.76]
Sweet Pickled Spring Ginger

［材料］

新しょうが…150g、酢…100cc、砂糖…50g、塩…小1/2

❶ 新しょうがは薄くスライスする。鍋で熱湯から1分間茹でる。

❷ 茹でたら冷ます。

❸ 鍋に調味料を入れて、一度沸騰させる。粗熱が取れたらしょうがを漬ける。食べ頃は3〜4日後から。1年は保存可能。

• 150 grams spring ginger, thinly sliced
• 100 ml vinegar
• 50 grams sugar
• 1/2 tsp salt

❶ In a pot, boil the spring ginger for a minute. Drain the water and let the ginger cool.

❷ In a pot, heat the vinegar, sugar, and salt and let it come to a boil.

❸ Once ❷ cools down, add ❶ and pickle for 3-4 days. It can be preserved up to a year.

9. 焼きそば [p.87]
Yakisoba

［材料］

焼きそば麺…2人分、キャベツ…3枚、中濃ソース…大4、

9

10

サラダ油…大1/2
❶ 麺に熱湯をかける。キャベツは
せん切りにする。
❷ フライパンにサラダ油をひいて
キャベツを炒めてから、麺を入れ
て炒め、ソースを絡める。

- -

• 2 servings yakisoba noodles
• 1/2 tbsp cooking oil, for the
pan
• 3 leaves cabbage, julienned
• 4 tbsp semi-thick
Worcestershire sauce

- -

❶ Pour boiling water over the
noodles.
❷ Heat a pan with the oil,
stir-fry the cabbage and add
noodles and sauce.

10. 山形のだっし [p.101]

Yamagata Dasshi

[材料]
なす…1本、おくら…4本、みょう
が…1本、大葉…5枚、きゅうり…
1本、市販のめんつゆ…大3
❶ 全ての野菜を細かく切り、市販
のめんつゆで合わせる。
＊食べきれない場合は冷蔵庫で2～3日保
存可能。

- -

• 1 eggplant, finely chopped
• 4 okras, finely chopped
• 1 myoga, finely chopped
• 1 cucumber, finely chopped
• 5 ooba leaves, finely chopped
• 3 tbsp mentsuyu

- -

❶ Mix all ingredients into the
mentsuyu sauce. Leftovers can
be kept in the fridge for 2-3
days.

11. ひじきの煮物 [p.111]

Simmered Hijiki

［材料］

乾燥ひじき…10g、人参…50g、油揚げ…1/2枚、しいたけ…2個、だし汁…1カップ、醤油…大2、みりん…小1、砂糖…小2、酒…大1、サラダ油…小1

❶ ひじきはさっと洗い、たっぷりの水に15分浸して戻し、食べやすい大きさに切る。人参はせん切り、油揚げは熱湯をかけて油抜きし、1cmに切る。しいたけは薄切りにする。

❷ 鍋にサラダ油をひいて、人参、ひじき、しいたけを炒める。油揚げを入れて炒め、だし汁を加え、中火に。煮立ったら調味料を入れる。

❸ 落とし蓋をして、水気がなくなるまで中火で煮る。

- 10 grams dried hijiki
- 1/2 slice deep-fried tofu
- 1 tsp cooking oil, for the pot
- 50 grams carrots, julienned
- 2 shiitake, thinly sliced
- 1 cup dashi
- 2 tbsp soy sauce
- 1 tsp mirin
- 2 tsp sugar
- 1 tbsp sake

❶ Wash and soak hijiki in water for 15 minutes, then cut into small pieces. Pour boiling water on the deep-fried tofu, then cut into 1 cm pieces.

❷ Heat the oil in a pot over low heat and cook the carrots, hijiki, shiitake, and deep-fried tofu. Add the dashi and raise the heat to medium and bring

to a boil. Add the soy sauce, mirin, sugar, and sake.
❸ Cover the hijiki with a drop-lid and let the pot simmer until the water is absorbed.

12. ハンバーグ [p.134]

Salisbury Steak

［材料］
豚牛合い挽き肉…200g、玉ねぎ…50g、パン粉…大1、牛乳…大2、卵…1/2個、塩…小1/4、こしょう…少々、バター…小1、サラダ油…小2、ソース（トマトケチャップ…大2、ウスターソース…大2、赤ワイン…大1）

❶ 玉ねぎをみじん切りにして、バターで透き通るまで炒める。
❷ パン粉を牛乳で浸し、粗熱のとれた玉ねぎと合い挽き肉と一緒に合わせ、調味料、卵も加え、よく練る。

❸ 二等分にして丸め、手に打ちつけるようにして空気を抜く。楕円形にして、中央を指でくぼませる。
❹ フライパンに油をひいて、中火から強火で片面を焦げ目がつくまでしっかりと焼く。ひっくり返して、中火から弱火にしながら、蓋をして7分焼く。
❺ ハンバーグに竹串をさし、肉汁が透明になったら、ソースの調味料を入れて煮詰める。

- -

- 1 tsp butter, for the pan
- 50 grams onion, minced
- 1 tbsp bread crumbs
- 2 tbsp milk
- 100 grams ground beef
- 100 grams ground pork
- 1/2 egg
- 1/4 tsp salt
- 1/4 tsp pepper
- 2 tsp cooking oil, for the pan

For the sauce:
- 2 tbsp ketchup
- 2 tbsp Worcestershire sauce
- 1 tbsp red wine

❶ Heat the butter in a pan over medium heat and stir-fry the onion until traslucent. Let it cool.

❷ In a bowl, add bread crumbs, milk, ❶, ground pork and beef, egg, salt, and pepper. Knead.

❸ Separate ❷ in half and form into two burgers. Release air pockets by slapping the burgers back and forth between the hands. Shape them into oval patties and make a dent in the center.

❹ Heat the oil in a pan over medium heat and cook the patties. Gradually raise to high heat and lightly burn the surface until thoroughly cooked. Flip the patties over and turn down the heat to low heat and cover the pan with a lid. Cook for 7 minutes.

❺ Stick a skewer into the patties. If the juice runs clear, add the ingredients for the sauce into the pan and simmer. If not, cook further.

13. ローストビーフ ［p.144］
Roast Beef

［材料］

ローストビーフ用牛肉…500g、塩…小1、こしょう…適宜、醤油…大3、レモン汁…1個分、練り辛子…小2、サラダ油…小2

❶ 肉に塩こしょうをする。フライパ

13

14

ンを熱し油を薄くひいて、肉に焦
げ目をつける。
❷ アルミホイルに❶を包み、200
度のオーブンで10分焼く。熱いう
ちに醤油、レモン汁、練り辛子を
まぜた調味料に漬け、最低3時間
は漬けこむ。

- -

• 2 tsp cooking oil, for the pan
• 500 grams beef rump,
seasoned with salt and pepper
• 1 tsp salt
• 1/2 tsp pepper
• 3 tbsp soy sauce
• Juice of 1 lemon
• 2 tsp karashi paste

❶ Heat the cooking oil in a pan
over medium heat and brown
the meat.
❷ Wrap ❶ with foil and cook in
oven at 200 °C for 10 minutes.

❸ In a bowl, mix the soy sauce,
lemon juice, and karashi paste.
While still hot, soak ❷ in the
mixture. Let it sit for at least 3
hours.

14. 甘酢れんこん [p.145]
Sweet Vinegar Lotus Root

[材料]
れんこん…100g、酢…大1、砂糖
…小2、塩…少々
❶ 2mmに切ったれんこんを熱湯で
さっとゆがく。
❷ 熱いうちに調味料に浸し、一晩
漬ける。

- -

• 100 grams lotus root, sliced
into 2 mm pieces
• 1 tbsp vinegar
• 2 tsp sugar
• 1/2 tsp salt

- -

❶ Blanch the lotus root.
❷ In a bowl, mix the sweet vinegar, sugar, and salt.
❸ While still hot, soak ❷ in the mixture. Let it sit overnight.

15. 肉味噌 [p.166]

Nikumiso
（miso flavored ground pork）

[材料]
豚ひき肉…125g、味噌…大3、白味噌…大1、醤油…小2、砂糖…大1.5、みりん…大3、酒…大1.5、おろしニンニク…小1、一味唐辛子…少々、サラダ油…小1、ごま油…小1

❶ 鍋にサラダ油を熱し、豚ひき肉を中火で水分がなくなるまでよく炒める。
❷ ごま油以外の調味料をまぜ❶に加える。照りがでるまで木べらでかきまぜながら弱火で炒める。
❸ 最後にごま油を加える。

- 1 tsp cooking oil, for the pan
- 125 grams ground pork
- 3 tbsp miso
- 1 tbsp white miso
- 2 tsp soy sauce
- 1 1/2 tbsp sugar
- 3 tbsp mirin
- 1 1/2 tbsp sake
- 1 tsp garlic, ground
- 1/2 tsp ichimi togarashi
- 1 tsp sesame oil

❶ Heat the cooking oil in a pot over medium heat and cook the ground pork until water disappears.
❷ Add all the ingredients except the sesame oil into ❶, lower the heat and mix with a wooden spoon until glossy.
❸ Add the sesame oil in ❷.

15

16

16. 薄焼き卵 ［p.167］

Usuyaki Tamago（Thin Omelette）

［材料2枚分］

卵…1個、塩…少々、砂糖…少々、
サラダ油…小1

❶ 卵に塩と砂糖を入れ、よく溶き
ほぐす。

❷ フライパンを弱火で熱し、熱く
なったら油をひく。余分な油はキッ
チンペーパーで取り除く。

❸ ぬれ布巾の上にフライパンをの
せて、粗熱を取る。❶の半分をフ
ライパンに流し、薄く全体に伸ば
す。

❹ 弱火で熱し、表面が乾いたら、
取り出してザルなどに広げて冷ま
す。

❶ In a bowl, add salt and sugar
into the egg and mix well.

❷ Heat a pan over low heat
and add the cooking oil. Use
paper towel to spread and
remove excess oil.

❸ Place the pan on a damp
cloth or paper towel to remove
excess heat.

❹ Pour half of ❶ into the pan
and spread it thin across the
surface.

❺ When the surface of the egg
dries, remove the omelette and
let it rest on a sieve. Repeat
with remaining half egg.

（makes two）

- a pinch of salt
- 1/2 tsp sugar
- 1 egg, beaten
- 1 tsp cooking oil, for the pan

おにぎりをお弁当につめる
HOW TO PACK A BENTO

おにぎりといえば、お弁当ですが、形をくずさずに持ち運びをするのは意外とむずかしいもの。おにぎりを上手にお弁当にする方法を考えてみました。

Onigiri is portable and perfect for bentos. Still, many of us have eagerly opened our bentos only to find the onigiri crushed or deformed. Here are some bento packing tricks to securely carry your onigiri.

まずは、タッパーに三角おにぎりを対称にねかせて、隙間におかずを入れて動くのを防ぐ入れ方Ⓐ。おにぎりに接する部分には、おかずの味や色がうつらないように、キュウリや大葉などをはさみます。

ペットボトルホルダーに縦に入れる方法もありますⒷ。縦に長

いのでおにぎりを3個以上入れることができます。保冷剤を入れると野外でも安心です。

昔からおにぎりに使われてきた、竹皮**C**や竹籠**D**を使う方法もあります。通気性もよく、おにぎりがべとつきません。

Symmetrically place in a Tupperware, two triangular onigiri and fill the empty spaces with okazu (side dishes in Japanese) to keep everything in place **A**. Create "screens" along the onigiri using greens or cucumbers to avoid the taste and colors from blending.

Water bottle holders **B** are also convenient for carrying onigiri. Usually it can hold up to 3 onigiri. Include an ice pack when bringing it to outdoor events.

The traditional ways of using bamboo sheaths **C** and bamboo baskets **D** keep the onigiri aerated and prevents them from becoming clammy.

アルミホイルでくるんでから新聞紙でつつむと、食べ終わったら捨てるだけの手間いらず**E**。

平らにしたおにぎりをラップで四角につつみ、サンドイッチのように持っていく方法もあります**F**。その他に、おにぎり専用のお弁当箱**G**もあります。下段にはおかずを、上段におにぎりを入れるタイプや、おにぎりを1個だけ入れる専用ケース**H**も。オリジナルのつつみ方を考えるのも楽しいでしょう。

E

Alternatively, wrapping them in aluminum foil and then with newspaper **E** will do as well. For a flat or square onigiri, simply wrap it in saran wrap **F**. It's onigiri, sandwich style. You can also find bento boxes designed for onigiri **G**. Some are double deckers to keep the okazu on the bottom and the onigiri on top. There are even cases to carry a single onigiri **H**. Have fun exploring unique ways to pack your onigiri!

おにぎりを冷凍保存
HOW TO KEEP LEFTOVER ONIGIRI

炊きたてのご飯が余ったときなどは、おにぎりを作って冷凍保存しておくと、美味しく食べられます。

When you are left with excess onigiri, preserve it by deep-freezing.

❶ おにぎりを1個ずつしっかりとラップにつつみ、タッパーなどに入れて冷凍します。

Individually wrap the onigiri with saran wrap, and store in a Tupperware or container to avoid freezer burn.

❷ おにぎりの大きさにもよりますが、解凍するときは、電子レンジ（500W）で3〜4分、蒸し器で5〜8分くらいが目安です。

Defrost an onigiri by heating it in the microwave（500W）for 3-4 minutes, or 5-8 minutes in a steamer. The time it takes to defrost an onigiri will depend on its size.

写真上：ふりふり手まりずし　3連手まりずし
カップ、写真左下：ちゅーぼーず！お弁当
応援！おにぎり型（俵）、写真右下：ちゅー
ぼーずおにぎり型丸6個

おにぎり作りに役立つグッズ
Useful Tools for Easy Onigiri

ご飯をつめて、蓋をするだけでミニおにぎりが簡単にできるも
のや、振るだけでまん丸な手まり形ができるもの。おにぎり作
りが楽しくできるグッズがいろいろ。お弁当作りやパーティーに
も活躍。作って楽しい、食べて楽しい、おにぎりタイムを！

There are many tools designed to make onigiri-making easy and fun. From presses
that produce miniature onigiri to shakers that form perfectly round balls, the list of
useful onigiri inventions goes on. With these tools, you're bound to have fun while
making creative onigiri for bentos and parties!

INGREDIENT GLOSSARY

aonori	dried green laver or seaweed in powder form. Used as flavoring for Okonomiyaki, Yakisoba, and Takoyaki. [⇒p27, 70, 94]
beni shoga	thin strips of ginger pickled in red plum vinegar. Used as a condiment for Gyudon, Okonomiyaki, Yakisoba, and Takoyaki. [⇒p.27, 46, 94]
daikon	Japanese or Chinese white radish. Grated raw daikon has digestive enzymes and is used commonly as a condiment. [⇒p.128, 155]
dashi	Japanese broth made by soaking kombu, cured bonito flakes, dried fish, or shiitake mushrooms. It is a fundamental ingredient for Japanese cuisine. [⇒p.122, 180, 192, 196, 197]
dasshi	minced summer vegetables such as eggplants, cucumbers, and okras seasoned with dashi and soy sauce. Originally from Yamagata prefecture in Japan, dasshi is most commonly served over rice, soba, or with tofu. [⇒p.101, 179]
denbu	a sweet, pink-flaked condiment made from seasoned ground fish. Popular in the springtime for its color, it is used as garnish for sushi rolls and other dishes. [⇒p.70]
doubanjiang	Chinese chili bean paste made with fermented broad beans, soybeans, rice, salt, and spices. It is the heart of Sichuan cuisine. [⇒p.172]
edamame	young soybeans, often boiled in the pods and salted. Known as a beer's best friend, it is the most popular Japanese "otsumami" (drinking

snacks). Precooked frozen edamame can be found in stores. [⇒p74, 98, 113, 126]

egoma oil	oil made from perilla seed. Rich in omega-3 fatty acids, it helps control high cholesterol. [⇒p103, 203]
enoki	mushrooms with long white stems and tiny caps. The texture is crisp and the taste is sweet. It pairs particularly well with soupy dishes such as nabe and sukiyaki. [⇒p.62, 129]
eringi	mushrooms with thick, meaty stems, also known as king trumpet mushrooms. The taste is sweet and buttery. [⇒p129, 153]
gochujang	Korean fermented red pepper paste made from red chile peppers, glutinous rice, and soybeans. It is sweet, pungent, and mildly hot with a thick texture. [⇒p.165]
gunkan-style	gunkan means "battleship" in Japanese. It is usually associated with a special style of sushi resembling a boat: an oval clump of rice with a strip of nori wrapped around its perimeter to form a vessel filled with toppings. [⇒p30, 155]
hijiki	black shredded seaweed, usually sold dry. Rich in minerals, iron, and fiber, hijiki has been called a "seaweed vegetable" and has become a staple ingredient in macrobiotic cooking. [⇒p111, 180]
ikura	salmon roe. Usually a shade of florescent orange with a tint of red, ikura tastes fresh and salty. The saltiness of the ikura perfectly matches the rice, making it a sushi favorite. Commonly consumed

	as "ikuradon" (ikura served over rice). [⇒p.57]
jyako	dried salted baby sardines. Naturally preserved, it can be stored in the freezer and can be used as a topping on rice, omelettes, salads, and other dishes. [⇒p.84]
kanikama	artificial crab meat made of surimi (white fish) that resembles crab legs. Often used in California sushi rolls. [⇒p.79]
karaage	Japanese deep-fried chicken. Marinated in soy sauce, sake, and ginger, the karaage stays juicy even after it cools. It is one of the most popular okazu (side dish) in Japan. [⇒p.48, 174]
karashi paste	Japanese mustard made from ground mustard seed and horseradish. Usually sold in powder or paste form, karashi is used as a condiment or as a seasoning on dishes such as tonkatsu and oden. [⇒p.58, 144, 183]
kari kari ume	tiny crunchy umeboshi made by pickling young ume in salt. The word "kari kari" means "crunchy". They taste sweet, tart, and salty. [⇒p.83]
kazunoko	herring roe, dried and then pickled in salt. Usually yellow, it has a unique texture that is firm and rubbery, yet crunchy. Since "kazu" means number and "ko" means child in Japanese, it is traditionally consumed in Japan on New Years to wish for many healthy children. [⇒p.91]
kimchi	traditional Korean fermented vegetable pickles, usually made of Chinese cabbage or radish. [⇒p.150]

kinoko	collective term for Japanese mushrooms. They add earthy flavors and fragrance to Japanese cuisine. [⇒p.129]
kinpira	chopped burdock and carrot sautéed and simmered in sugar, soy sauce, and mirin. A traditional Japanese home cooking recipe. [⇒p.54, 176]
kombu	dried kelp. Full of minerals, nutrients, and umami, kombu is used extensively in Japanese cuisine for making soup stock. Store in airtight containers away from sunlight and moisture. [⇒p.123, 192, 197, 198]
konnyaku	a jelly-like product made from a root plant in the taro family called Konnyaku. On its own it has very little taste, but konnyaku is popular as a healthy diet food, containing almost no calories. It also comes in a threaded form. [⇒p51, 176]
mapo tofu	Sichuan-style bean curd set in a spicy chili bean sauce. Usually cooked with fermented black beans and minced meat such as pork or beef. [⇒p.44, 172]
mehari	a rice ball wrapped in pickled takana, a rare type of mustard green. Originally from the rural Kumano region in Japan, mehari is now popular throughout the country. [⇒p162]
mentaiko	fresh pollock eggs marinated in salt and red chile peppers. The red, spicy roe is sold in its natural membrane or in jars. To use, slice open the sac

	and scroop out the eggs. It makes a great onigiri filling, but the most popular way to eat it is to mix it into spaghetti to make mentaiko spaghetti. [⇒p.40]
mentsuyu	a multipurpose noodle sauce, perfect for dipping cold soba, somen noodles, tempura, and more. [⇒p.179]
mirin	sweet rice wine with a lower alcohol content than sake. An essential condiment for Japanese cuisine, it adds a mild sweetness and luster to the ingredients and masks the smell of fish with its aroma. [⇒p.41, 45, 122, 135, 165, 169, 173, 176, 177, 180, 184, 195, 197, 199, 200]
miso	thick soybean paste, made by fermenting rice or barley (koji) and soybeans with salt. It can be used for sauces or pickling vegetables and meats, but is most commonly mixed into dashi stock to serve as miso soup. [⇒p.26, 27, 45, 61, 135, 184, 196, 201]
myoga	a deciduous perennial plant, sometimes called zingiber mioga. Similar to ginger, it has a refreshing taste. The flower buds and shoots are usually shredded and used as a garnish for miso soup, soba, and tempura. [⇒p.179]
natto	fermented soybeans. Despite its pungent smell and slimy texture, natto is highly nutritious and rich in protein and typically served for breakfast. [⇒p.50]

nikumiso	minced pork seasoned with soybean paste. Nikumiso can serve as a topping for steamed rice or noodles or can simply be wrapped in lettuce. [⇒p.166, 184]
nori tsukudani	nori seaweed jam simmered with soy sauce, sugar, sake, and mirin. Its strong salty kombu flavor makes a perfect topping for a bowl of rice. [⇒p.168]
okaka	shaved katsuobushi (dried bonito flakes) tossed in soy sauce. Popularly used as a topping on pickles, tofu, okonomiyaki, or as furikake seasoning for rice. It can also be used to make dashi soup stock. [⇒p.56, 61, 78]
ooba	Japanese perilla leaves. A member of the mint family, ooba has a strong citrus flavor and a minty fragrance. [⇒p.27, 76, 83, 144, 163, 168, 179]
osekihan	a traditional celebratory dish made from azuki beans and sticky rice. Sekihan translates to "red rice" in Japanese because the azuki beans color the rice. [⇒p.130]
ponzu	a citrus-based sauce containing soy sauce, vinegar, and katsuobushi (dried bonito flakes). Its sour, sweet, and salty flavor makes it a perfect dipping sauce for shabu shabu and nabe. [⇒p.159]
sake	Japanese rice wine. [⇒p.41, 45, 62, 122, 123, 124, 128, 129, 169, 172, 174, 176, 180, 184, 194, 196, 197, 200]
senbei	Japanese rice crackers. A traditional snack that comes in all shapes, sizes, and flavors. [⇒p.114]

shibazuke

chopped vegetables such as cucumber and eggplant pickled in ume vinegar, salt, and red shiso leaves. The Kyoto-style pickles are bright purple in color and dyed by the shiso leaves. [⇒p.50]

shiitake

the most popular Japanese mushrooms, with tough stems. They can be found in gourmet markets across the country. Also sold dry, they can be reconstituted in water for a rich dashi stock. [⇒p147, 180, 192]

shimeji

straw-colored mushrooms with small brown rounded caps. The versitile, rich, and nutty flavor adds a round taste to takikomi-gohan and vegetable stir-fry, among many other dishes. [⇒p129]

shiokombu

strips of kombu that have been boiled in soy sauce, dried and then cut into pieces. Commonly used as an accompaniment to rice, shiokombu is the perfect combination of salt and umami. [⇒p.74]

shirataki

white konnyaku noodles made from devil's tongue yam. The word "shirataki" means "white waterfall." Commonly used in one-pot meals such as nabe or sukiyaki. [⇒p.173, 199]

shumai

small steamed pork dumplings. Originally served as dim sum in China, these small dumplings are easy to make and keep well in the freezer, making it a popular okazu (side dish) for bentos. [⇒p.58, 177]

sukiyaki	a traditional one-pot meal cooked at the table as you eat. Main ingredients include thinly sliced beef, vegetables, and shirataki and are simmered in a soy sauce based soup. Cooked differently depending on the regions in Japan. [⇒p.46, 173, 193, 198]
takanazuke	pickled takana（a rare type of mustard green）. [⇒p.38, 115, 154, 162]
takuan	yellow pickled radish. The most common type of tsukemono (pickles) in traditional Japanese cuisine. [⇒p.50, 106]
tarako	salted pollock roe. It can be eaten raw as a paste or cooked for a firm texture. It has a strong salty flavor. [⇒p.40, 55, 77]
tsukudani	small seafood, meat, or seaweed simmered in soy sauce and mirin. The process helps to preserve the ingredients. The name comes from its origin, the island Tsukudajima in Tokyo. [⇒p.110, 168]
umeboshi	Japanese salty pickled plums. Sun-dried and then pickled in shiso leaves with salt for over a year, the umeboshi plum is extremely sour and tart. Ideal for sushi, rice, and onigiri. High in citric acid, it has been valued for centuries as a digestive aid and is commonly served in porridges to cure the common cold. When mixed with shochu, the umeboshi is used as a way to prevent hangovers. [⇒p.39, 61, 81, 194, 199, 201]
umezu	the brine produced from making umeboshi. A

	dash of umezu in sushi rice or other marinated dishes will infuse a fruity aroma and boost the saltiness. [⇒p.157]
unagi	freshwater eel broiled in soy sauce based sweet sauces. Rich in proteins and vitamins, it is believed to sustain stamina. For this reason, unagi is most frequently consumed during the hottest days of summer to overcome the heat. [⇒p.156]
usuyaki tamago	Japanese paper-thin egg crepe. Often used to wrap rice in many different ways or to make temari sushi. It can also be julienned into kinshi tamago to be used as garnish. [⇒p.167, 185]
wakame	a kind of seaweed, often sold dried. It has a soft texture and a subtle sweet flavor. Most commonly served in soups and salads. [⇒p.79]
wasabi	Japanese horseradish, often used for sushi and sashimi. When consumed, a short intense burn travels through the sinuses. Grating fresh wasabi right before serving will optimize its unique and pungent flavor. [⇒p.47, 60]
yakisoba	a Japanese-style chow mein typically made by stir-frying egg noodles with vegetables and pork. It is easy to make and can be found at festivals and street vendors. [⇒p87, 178, 192]
yakitori	barbecued chicken on a skewer. Almost every part of the chicken including the thighs, skin, and liver can be used for yakitori. It can be served

	with salt and lemon juice or with a sauce made of mirin, sake, soy sauce, and sugar. They make a great "otsumami" when washed down with beer. [⇒p.41]
yukari	powdered seasoning made of the dried red shiso leaves used to produce umeboshi. Usually served by sprinkling over rice, pasta, and salads. [⇒p.43]
yuzu	a small yellow citrus fruit with a tart and acidic taste. The rind is frequently used for a sweet, floral fragrance. [⇒p.160, 201]
yuzukosho	a fermented paste made from chile peppers, yuzu peel, and salt. Usually used as a condiment for one-pot meals such as nabe and shabu shabu as well as miso soup and sashimi. [⇒p.85]
zha cai	commonly known as "Sichuan preserved vegetable," zha cai is made by salting, pressing, and fermenting the stem of Brassica juncea, a variety of mustard greens. Crunchy, salty, and sour, it is often used as relish for rice, tofu, and steamed buns. [⇒p.91]
zuke	Japanese cooking method for soaking or marinating in soy sauce. [⇒p.60]

この本で使用したもの PRODUCT LIST

- ●米 Rice
  たかたのゆめ http://takatanoyume.big-apple.info/

- ●塩 Sea Salt
  能登 わじまの海塩 [⇒p.19]
  株式会社美味と健康 http://www.wajimanokaien.com/

- ●焼き海苔 Nori Seaweed／オリーブ海苔 Olive Nori [⇒p.72, 158]
  石巻元気商店 http://store.shopping.yahoo.co.jp/otr-ishinomaki/

- ●押し麦 Rolled Barley [⇒p.55]／もち麦 Mochi Mugi（Waxy Barley）[⇒p.81]
  16穀米 Jurokkoku (16 Grains) [⇒p.88, 98]／麦茶 Premium Barley Tea [⇒p.126]
  株式会社はくばく http://www.hakubaku.co.jp/

- ●豆苗 Pea Sprouts [⇒p.95]
  ブロッコリースーパースプラウト Broccoli Super Sprouts [⇒p.84]
  株式会社村上農園 http://www.murakamifarm.com/

- ●特殊三分搗き米「芽ぐみ米」
  Special Three percent milled-rice Megumi rice [⇒p.73]
  東京フーズクリエイト http://www.tokyofoods.jp/

- ●えごま油 Egoma Oil（Perilla Oil）[⇒p.102]
  （株）オーサン http://www.o-san.co.jp/

- ●POPSO blue スパイスオイル Spice Oil [⇒p.156]
  VENUS 8 http://www.popso.jp/

- ●お重、敷物 Lacquer ware boxes and place mats [⇒p.64, 70, 108, 130, 148]
  OJIGI TOKYO http://www.ojigi.jp/

- ●おにぎり作りに役立つグッズ Useful Tools for Easy Onigiri [⇒p.191]
  貝印株式会社 http://www.kai-group.com

おわりに　CLOSING

101人いれば、101通りのそれぞれ好みのおにぎりがあり、誰にでも懐かしくちょっと微笑んでしまうような「おにぎり」の思い出があります。

私のおにぎりの思い出は中学の時、入院中の母に代わり祖母が作ってくれたのりで巻いただけのおにぎり。
友だちのピンクや黄色のカラフルな可愛いおにぎりがうらやましく……ちょっと悲しかった思い出があります。

地方創生の「熱中小学校」プロジェクトに関わり、各地方をまわると、ご当地おにぎりに出会います。自慢のおにぎり談議が止まりません。
また、海外でおにぎりイベントを開催すると、食べたことはないけれど、日本のアニメでおにぎりは知っている、ぜひ作って食べたい、との声を多数聞いてきました。

おにぎりにはなぜだか、手のぬくもりがいっぱい詰まっていて、おにぎりを食べるとつくった人の気持ちをいただいているような気持ちになり、不思議と元気が出てきます。
みなさんの思い出のおにぎりはなんでしょうか。
1つのおにぎりに思い出がつまっている……たかがおにぎり、されどおにぎりです。

日本の家庭料理では欠かせないおにぎり、日本の心……ソウルフードです。

Easy、simple、healthy の3拍子そろった手軽なおにぎり。
おにぎりで世界を結ぶ……私の小さな外交もここからスタートです。

山田玲子

If 101 people make 101 onigiri, each will have their own onigiri story.

My story takes me back to middle school, when my grandmother made onigiri for me while my mother was ill.
Hers was always very simple — a plain rice ball wrapped in nori seaweed.
I remember looking over enviously at my friends' onigiri, cute and colorful pink and yellow rice balls. Now it's all a bittersweet memory.

I had the opportunity to travel around Japan when I participated in a rural community revitalization project called "Necchu Elementary School," where I discovered many unique local onigiri. The locals would proudly boast that their onigiri were the best of them all and it seemed there was no end to this passionate onigiri debate.
Even when I hosted events abroad, many people told me they had always wanted to try onigiri which they learned of through their favorite anime characters.

There seems to be something magical about onigiri.
Packed by two hands, somehow, it embodies the warmth of the person who made it.
It's almost as if you can "feel" the love when you eat it.
It's surprisingly invigorating.
What is your onigiri story?
It may be just onigiri, but it's so much more.

Easy, simple and healthy, onigiri is a staple of conventional Japanese soul food.
Join me in spreading the circle of onigiri diplomacy today, one onigiri at a time.

Reiko Yamada

Staff Credit

編集	戸塚貴子
英語翻訳	水野菜生
ブックデザイン	小久保由美
写真	難波純子
	山田玲子
	(p.64-65, p.70-71, p.92-93, p108-109, p130-131, p136-137, p148-149, p170-171)
翻訳協力	トーマス・ミラー
	ジェニファー・シット
料理助手	福原香織
モデル	山下晴 (p.3)

本作品はポット出版より2014年4月に刊行されました。

山田玲子 やまだ・れいこ

クッキングアドヴァイザー。フェリス女学院大学卒。
1995年から浜田山の自宅で料理教室「Salon de R」を主宰し、家庭料理を中心に、おもてなしのコーディネートを楽しく大胆に伝授する笑いあふれるレッスンが人気。また、男子、父子料理教室などを通じて家庭での食の力の向上を伝えている。「食は一番身近な外交」と、NYやシンガポールなどでも料理教室・イベントを開催し、食を通じた国際交流にも力を注ぐ。著書に『和ごはん101』英訳付き（ポット出版）、『NY発！ サラダBOWLレシピ』『定年ごはん』（共に大和書房）など。

Reiko Yamada

Reiko Yamada is a cooking adviser. A graduate of Ferris University, she began teaching cooking in 1995 by hosting workshops, "Salon de R," in her home in Tokyo. Her dynamic workshops that cover topics like home cooking and dinner hosting have built a strong following of students who attend her class for a fun and creative experience. She also actively promotes men's participation in cooking through her lessons.

Championing the idea of food as the most basic form of diplomacy, she hosts workshops at home and abroad, in cities such as New York and Singapore, as a means of intercultural communication.

Publications include *Wagohan: The ABCs of Japanese Cooking* (2017), *Everyday Onigiri* (2014), *Salad Bowl Recipes from NY Style* (2015), and *Teinen Gohan* (2018).

おにぎりレシピ101

著者　山田玲子
©2019 Reiko Yamada, Printed in Japan
2019年4月15日第1刷発行

発行者　佐藤 靖
発行所　大和書房
東京都文京区関口1-33-4 〒112-0014
電話 03-3203-4511
フォーマットデザイン　鈴木成一デザイン室
印刷　歩プロセス
製本　ナショナル製本

ISBN978-4-479-30758-7
乱丁本・落丁本はお取り替えいたします。
http://www.daiwashobo.co.jp